C S Lewis

Author of *Mere Christianity*

Sam Wellman

A Barbour Book

Other books in the "Heroes of the Faith" series:

John Bunyan
Fanny Crosby
Jim Elliot
Billy Graham
David Livingstone
D. L. Moody
Martin Luther
Samuel Morris
John Newton
Charles Spurgeon
Corrie ten Boom
Sojourner Truth
John Wesley

©MCMXCVII by Sam Wellman

ISBN 1-55748-979-3

Published by Barbour & Company, Inc.
            P.O. Box 719
            Uhrichsville, Ohio 44683
            http://www.barbourbooks.com

Member of the
Evangelical Christian
Publishers Association

Printed in the United States of America.

C S
Lewis

To the Pen-Inktons
of McPherson, Kansas

one

No-Man's-Land

"A new officer's coming, Lieutenant Lewis," informed Sergeant Ayres.

Worst luck! thought Lieutenant C.S. Lewis of the 3rd Somerset Light Infantry, who did not feel like a welcoming presence that day in France. The German artillery, which had been dropping in shells more than usual all day, made him feel hunkered down. Rumors of mustard gas from the north had driven him to clutch his gas mask, and now his fingers ached. Worse yet, the scuttlebutt that approximately fifteen German divisions were ready to assault Arras, which lay directly behind Lieutenant Lewis, niggled his tired mind. Worst of all, as ghastly as the trenches were, he was not fit to lead men against the Germans in the open. He would have to lean on Sergeant Ayres like he always did. No, he certainly didn't feel like a welcoming committee for any new officer.

Sighing, he studied the entrance of the communications trench. Suddenly the grimy face of a sergeant and the bright face of a new officer appeared at the entrance above him. A barely audible gasp revealed the officer's sudden realization that he was on a precipice. "We've come to a new trench, and this one must be another ten feet deep," he chirped.

"At least ten feet deep, sir," replied his sergeant. "We've been walking in a communications trench. This is a real trench. We're at the front line, sir."

"My legs are rubber," confessed the new officer, whose falsetto betrayed his youth. "Why is the communications trench so zigzagged? Seems an awful waste."

Lieutenant Lewis spoke up. "In case of a direct hit from artillery or a fusillade from small arms, we don't want the projectiles going up and down the whole straight-line trench killing every one of us, now do we?"

The new officer spotted Lieutenant Lewis and gulped. "Of course not, Lieutenant." He descended a ladder and thumped onto the boarded bottom of the trench. He blinked. "Say, don't I know you, old boy? Were you at Malvern school, by chance? Jack, is it?"

"Perhaps," replied Jack Lewis coldly, "but that means nothing here. Cricket is temporarily postponed."

The man took the hint and shut up about elite public schools. Jack Lewis saw no need to get friendly. When this new man died, it wouldn't be so hard for him to accept. How many of his new friends had been killed already? He had lost count. Besides, this time he really felt like he was going to get killed himself. He watched the new officer climb up on the fire step by a periscope.

"Hard to see through all the barbed wire," muttered the new officer, gawking through the periscope. "How far away are the krauts?"

Jack Lewis squirmed against the hard-packed sandbags at his back and waited for someone else to answer the new officer. He hated the word "kraut," which was short for sauerkraut, a common German dish. He didn't like the word "jerry" to indicate Germans either. Words were special to Jack. Even up here where a man might die any second, he guarded his language and chose his words with precision. Must a man become a sloppy pig simply because he lived in mud?

When no one volunteered to answer the new officer's question, Jack finally spoke up. "The distance across no-man's-land to the German trench? Fifty yards or so."

"But then shouldn't I be able to see. . .I do see a field-gray uniform and a soup-pot helmet! A kraut is walking along a trench over there! Careless bloke. I dare say I could plug him right in the head."

"Good idea," drawled Jack dryly. "Poke your head up and take a pot shot."

"Oh, I see. One of them might shoot at me first. I say then, better yet, why don't we lob a rifle grenade into their trench?"

Some one groaned, but Jack Lewis had to laugh. He had voiced the same words exactly to Sergeant Ayres back on Day One of his entry in this Great War. When had that been? Oh yes, it had been his nineteenth birthday, November 29, 1917, four and a half months back. Noticing that no sergeant seemed eager this gloomy day to answer the new officer, Jack decided he would be the one to set him straight.

"Once you start that business," instructed Jack crisply, "you'll get it back in kind."

The new officer was startled. "But aren't we supposed to kill the krauts?"

"Oh, don't worry. Death is a common commodity in the trenches and even almost guaranteed in that no man's land between our trenches and their trenches. You see, every inch of that hellish ground is covered not only by our machine guns but their machine guns too. Death is almost a certainty."

"So it's a stalemate?" concluded the new officer, amazed.

"Only until some wine-sipping, chain-smoking general back at HQ gets antsy over his *hors d'oeuvres* because no map tacks are being moved on his map," grumbled

Jack Lewis sourly, "and decides one of his tacks, which happens to be one of our battalions, should charge the Germans."

"You don't say. . ." the young officer quirked an eyebrow.

"Go warm yourself by one of the fires," intoned Jack, brother-like. "Pick yourself a nice wire bunk in some dugout. Eat some stew. Read a good book." Jack felt like adding, *Because any day now—if you don't croak on mustard gas first—a whole division of Germans is going to storm across that fifty yards and nothing our puny battalion can do will stop them because this is their very last chance to win this terrible war before the Americans build up an army of several million men.*

But Jack didn't feel mean enough. Truth was he himself was frightened numb, more scared than he had ever been. He watched the new officer squeeze past a traverse and disappear. Traverses were thick walls of sandbags perpendicular to the trench. They occurred about every ten yards and served the same tactical purpose as zigzagging. The enemy could not devastate an entire trench with an exploding shell or a fusillade of bullets.

"I know far too much about trenches and warfare," muttered Jack to himself.

No one had handled the war quite as Jack had. He knew how to keep the future in its place. As an Irish citizen, he hadn't been required to volunteer for the draft at all. Precisely what had motivated him to do that noble act he no longer remembered. Perhaps he had reasoned if he was going to take advantage of Oxford University in England he could jolly well fight for England. Or perhaps he had done it so he could call himself a Welshman as his father did. Or perhaps he had done it because since 1914 brother Warnie had been fighting for England somewhere in this quagmire too. For whatever reason, he had volunteered for the draft, then, duty done, he simply ignored the war.

While others related in trembling voices that the British had lost 200,000 men in only the first year of the war, Jack read fantasies by his hero George MacDonald. While others chattered endlessly about this and that awful battle, Jack digested Plato. When he finally had gotten drafted, it was as if he woke up to say, "Oh yes, the war. I'm ready, I suppose." Only when, on his first day on the front, he had heard a bullet scream by somewhere had intense reality pulsed through him. *This is war,* he had thought. *This is what Homer wrote about.*

He actually admired some things about the war. He didn't have to be a hypocrite and pretend he liked it as he had in public school. No one liked the war, and that fact united Jack with all the others. For the first time in his life he enjoyed the company of real men. It felt very good. Proper gentlemen talked about everything but themselves. If someone said he was a west country farmer or an Irishman or an Oxford student at Christ Church college, it seemed to make him less than a real man. A real man talked about things. A real man didn't complain. Yes, Jack Lewis liked the company of real men very much. Their laughter was music to his ears.

Another good thing happened. All his boyhood Jack had sported a face that looked insolent regardless of his thoughts. What was it? Lowered eyelids? Sneering lips? Snaky pupils? A slack jaw? He never actually knew, but he had heard the complaint too often and in too many different places not to know it was something concrete. Whatever, he knew now that he had lost it. Maybe when his boots had touched the bloody soil of France. . .

"Lewis!" called the familiar voice of Laurence B. Johnson, another lieutenant in Jack's battalion. "Take a break, old chap. I've found a splendid hole in the wall not far from

11

here." That was Johnson, always cheery.

"Lead the way then," ordered Jack.

After they entered a freshly dug hole lit by a candle and almost warm from the earth, Johnson said, "See, it's plenty large enough for a spirited chat. Big enough for three gentlemen, really. I say, isn't there a new officer hereabouts?"

"I sent him to get some stew," explained Jack with little interest. He threw aside his gas mask.

"Well, I'll round him up," Johnson stated purposefully.

And with that he darted out. Yes, that was Laurence B. Johnson. Generous. Hospitable. Yanked away from Oxford just as Jack had been. Johnson practiced virtues, even took them for granted. He actually believed in a Supreme Being of some sort. In spite of that Jack liked him very much. He liked him so much he felt the urge to imitate him, this scholar who could discuss things as sharply as Jack's old tutor, "Kirk," yet believed in the old-fashioned virtues of truthfulness and chastity. Jack resisted those things. There was no rational reason to desire such virtues, and less reason to believe them. Yet, why was he attracted to Johnson so much? And why was Jack's favorite writer, George MacDonald, something of a religious prig?

"We're back, Lewis," announced Johnson, interrupting Jack's thoughts.

The new officer followed Johnson inside. He was strangely subdued now, the reality of the front lines having drained all the "cheery-ho!" out of him. This was a hell no man could imagine beforehand, and the new officer must have been told this was a very slow day.

"Jack Lewis and I usually debate theism, Thorne," explained Johnson, who had learned the name of the new officer.

"The existence of God? Go ahead then," said Thorne. "I'll

listen. I'm afraid the day has dulled my brain too much to contribute anything very sharp." He sounded very depressed. Suddenly the earth shook and the candle went out. "What was that?" asked Thorne in a high-pitched voice.

"Just our own cannons," elaborated Jack dryly as Johnson lit the candle again. Dirt trickled from the ceiling. Matter-of-factly, Jack continued, "I once read a whole volume of Robert Browning while the candle was going out every four minutes from our own cannons."

"I believe Lewis here was on slippery ground last time we talked about theism," Johnson inserted perkily.

Jack stiffened for a good fight. "Just because I admitted 'mind' seems more like spirit than flesh?"

"Certainly, old chap," Johnson grinned.

"All right," Jack conceded, shaking his head, "I admitted that I resent very much that material things like bullets and such can extend their dominion over the mind, which seems to me the only source possible for 'beauty.' And I also admitted that beauty—which exists only in the mind—seems like some sort of spirit thing." Johnson was smiling. "You needn't derive such satisfaction," objected Jack. "That conclusion doesn't necessitate what you believe in."

But deep inside, Jack was in agony over this cosmic debate. A separate spirit world was one way to explain the "otherness" of certain things that had thrilled him so much his entire life—things like his brother Warnie's toy garden or the Northern myths. Weren't those thrills possibly due to the tiniest glimpse into that spirit world?

"You admitted far more than that last time," goaded Johnson.

"You mean my simple equation? Matter equals nature equals Satan?"

"Satan!" echoed Johnson. "You see how far you've

come, old chap?"

"Satan is just an invention of the Jews or other ancient civilizations."

Johnson's face was sober. "I believe in your heart, Lewis, you are a dualist already."

"What! Believe in two Supreme Beings? One evil and one good? Like William Blake did? Hardly." Jack added a quiet humph.

Deep inside though, he was thinking along those lines. All he would admit to himself so far, however, was that he possessed some tiny chip of some unthinking universal spirit. He just could not bring himself to believe in spiritual beings that might actively be poking people this way and prodding people that way. And yet, he could freely admit that the appetites of his flesh seemed to be counter to his conscious desire for beauty. Yes, to himself he truly seemed some kind of Frankenstein's monster created by Nature or Satan. Here he was, desiring beauty, all the while fighting off the same lusty desires Nature gives a loathsome beetle!

"Lewis is of all things, first and last, a book lover," announced Johnson breezily, perhaps sensing Lewis was cornered, tired, and confused. "Show us your latest, old chap."

Jack reached inside his heavy trench coat and pulled out a precious volume. "I'm reading *Middlemarch* by George Eliot right now."

Thorne perked up. "I say, I've been meaning to read Eliot some day myself. . ."

Jack pulled out another book. "I'm through with *The Memoirs of Benvenuto Cellini*. I've read it twice."

"I say!" exclaimed Thorne again. "Twice?" He gingerly took the book from Jack.

14

"Oh, Lewis reads a book over and over," added Johnson.

"Of course," Jack countered defensively. "Where on earth do people get the idea that you should read a book only once? If it's really good, you must savor it again and again."

Thorne blinked. "I say, Lewis, you've blanketed the margins with notes. And see here! You've made your own index in back." The new officer seemed humbled. "Actually, I would send for some of my own books, but they're a bit too thin. Never survive this place very long, I fear."

"I have just the solution for you!" declared Jack, warming to the subject. How he loved books! "The girl in Ovenell's Bookstore in Oxford put me on to it. If the volumes are too thin you have them bound together in good solemn half leather and strong boards."

"Capital idea," affirmed Thorne.

Suddenly an explosion clapped their ears like thunder and the dugout was plunged into darkness. . .

15

two

"Are we alive?" whispered the new officer, Thorne.

Someone struck a match. It was Johnson relighting the candle. Dirt rained softly down inside the dugout. Thorne squirmed, unsure how to react. Johnson blew out the match, expressionless. Jack sighed and slipped his precious *Middlemarch* back inside his trench coat.

"So much for civilization," Jack sighed as he picked up his gas mask. "We had better go out and see who we lost in this 'Valley of Humiliation.'"

"Jack, you're right," spouted Thorne almost hysterically, "we are in John Bunyan's 'Valley of Humiliation.' A taste of hell itself!"

Solemnly, the three young officers left the dugout and attended to their duties. Jack, reluctant to leave the dugout, mentally lingered. The new officer, Thorne, was all right after all. Didn't talk about himself. Listened. Even took Jack's *The Memoirs of Benvenuto Cellini*. Looked like he might well read it. They could discuss it later if Thorne or Jack didn't get themselves killed. Worst luck, Jack thought, that he had to go to war to find such congenial company, because the destruction of war itself was the ultimate degradation. The soggy wetness. The clammy ears and noses. The sweaty feet in awkward gum boots. The cave-ins. The constant stench of human waste. The flies and maggots. And most degrading of all, the near misses that weren't near misses for companions suddenly torn and bloody and maimed, crawling and grasping and moaning and whimpering to their last breath.

"Did Paddy go like that?" he muttered.

Grim thoughts made him remember Paddy Moore. Moore was from Clifton College, but he had come to Oxford for Officer Training. He had become Jack's roommate at Keble where they were quartering the trainees. Jack had thought Paddy Moore childish at first, far too trusting and outrageously virtuous, but he had grown to like Moore. He also liked Moore's mother and 11-year-old sister Maureen when they came down from Bristol to stay until Paddy shipped out. Mrs. Moore was bossy, generous, caring, gregarious, affectionate—an Irish lady completely devoid of English reserve. She took Jack under her wing right along with Paddy and Maureen. And she wore well. Jack's affection for her grew every day. So the promise he made to Paddy Moore when they shipped out in their separate battalions didn't seem like such an earthshaking one. After all, Paddy was the most certain of all the soldiers Jack knew that he was going to get out of the bloody war alive. But now Paddy was missing. His Rifle Brigade had taken the full brunt of the German attack in March.

Paddy is probably dead at this very moment, brooded Jack to himself, *and I promised to take care of his mother for life if anything happened to him!. . .Well, so what? I probably won't be alive myself in a day or two.* He squeezed through the next traverse. There he saw that one of the enlisted men had been downed by fragments from the shell that had just burst and forced the three officers out of their dugout. The soldier was gasping and whimpering. He must have been lying on top of his wound because he didn't look all that bad, yet he showed all the signs of a man dying. He was

Irish like Jack, but from his pained words, Jack knew this man had his Christ at the end. Jack Lewis had nothing. The enlisted man had the assurance of heaven. Jack Lewis had nothing.

It hadn't always been that way. . .

There had been a time when Jack's mother, Flora, was alive that he knew God was as real as the sunshine. Father, Mother, brother Warnie, and Jack had attended church regularly. They were called "Ulster Protestants" by the Catholics. Although they considered their church much freer of ritual than the Catholic Church, it was nevertheless a rigid church, never swerving one iota from the Book of Common Prayer. Only the short, uplifting sermon was not dictated. Jack remembered that his mother seemed as engrossed in quieting his boyish fidgeting as in following the service, but even as a small boy he knew his father, Albert, loved the ritual and the familiar prayers. Everything was laid out just as it should be.

Blimey, those days were a delight to remember. A right happy little boy he had been back in Ireland to be sure. One day he stomped his foot at his given name "Clive" and informed one and all from that day forward he was "Jacksy." Even Father laughed and, miracle of miracles, didn't use his favorite expression, "What nonsense!" but called him Jacksy for a while, then Jack. Older brother Warnie seemed stunned. He had considered not being called Warren quite a triumph. "Too late, Warnie, for some name really decent," needled Jack.

Once in a while as Jack stopped to ponder his own drawings of a noble frog in armor or a regal bunny, he caught his own reflection in the nursery window. He had a pensive oval face with a thatch of short brown hair. In a careless moment, he mistook his brother Warnie's squarish face for his own. Jack giggled. "Guess what, Warnie?"

"In a minute, Jack," mumbled Warnie. "Let me finish this paragraph."

"Paragraph? What are you writing?" quizzed Jack.

"*The Rajah's Land.*"

"You're writing a story about India?"

"Of course. One can't draw pictures all the time."

"But why not? That's exactly what we've done as far back as I can remember."

"Well, now I'm writing a story about my pictures."

Jack had to think about that. It seemed like from the beginning of time he had drawn pictures, even maps, of Animal-Land, but he had never written a story. The stories about Animal-Land just collected in his head. Suddenly he saw a carriage drawing up in front of their house.

"Look!" he cried. "It's Uncle William."

"Nooo," whined Warnie. "Why couldn't it be Uncle Joseph. Even Uncle Richard."

They were doomed, regardless of which uncle it was. No story of leprechauns from their nursemaid Lizzie tonight. They would be lucky to get half of *Peter Rabbit*. When Father, whom they secretly called Poodaytabird because of the funny way he said potato, had company he always "invited" the boys to listen to their manly conversation. And it had always the same subjects: business and politics, mostly politics.

"God forbid we get another Prime Minister like Gladstone," complained Albert later to Uncle William. "What nonsense!"

"Gladstone was a rogue and a fool," agreed Uncle William. "Home rule for the Irish? Ridiculous."

"Absolutely," agreed Albert.

Jack glanced at Warnie. Yes, Warnie remembered the exact conversation taking place before too. It was always the

19

same. The boys listened and tried to process the seeming contradictions in the conversations. Poodaytabird considered himself a Welshman, although his mother was a Gee from Liverpool in England. The boys lived in Ireland, but somehow their city of Belfast was like an English city, unless of course one considered himself Scotch like Uncle Augustus Hamilton and his sister Flora—who was the boys' mother. Yet Grandmother Hamilton was a Warren, a family that considered itself English. It was certainly complicated. Only their nursemaid Lizzie seemed really rooted in Ireland. "It's 1904," declared Uncle William as if that explained something.

"Perhaps you're right," acknowledged Poodaytabird. "Jack is only six and he has such a weak chest."

Jack had lost the thread of the conversation. Uncle William was trying to get Poodaytabird to do something, but Jack had not been paying attention. What did Jack's weak chest have to do with anything? And why did Warnie look worried? What were the two men talking about? Jack would have to ask Warnie later. In the meantime the men were talking about Poodaytabird's job as lawyer. Uncle William seemed to want Poodaytabird to run for office, whatever that meant. Poodaytabird shrugged; "It takes money." Now Jack had picked up the thread again. He had heard that conversation about running for office a dozen times before—at least.

Later in the nursery he blurted to Warnie, "Why did they talk about my weak chest?"

"Because Poodaytabird is worried about you catching cold, Small-Piggy-Bottom."

"So what, Arch-Piggy-Bottom?" countered Jack.

"He wants us to move outside Belfast where it's healthier—up toward the Holywood Hills where Uncle Joseph lives."

"What?. . .Move?. . .Change?"

Jack's fright seemed to affect Lizzie. She stayed to read the boys all of *Peter Rabbit*. But it wasn't enough. Jack had his worst kind of nightmare. He dreamed of beetles. They were so horrid. They had gnashing jaws. And their legs were covered with barbs. And they moved so much faster than Jack. And they chased him and crawled over his face all night. Oh, how Jack hated insects!

"Come out to the garden, and let's dig for a pot of gold," Warnie proposed the next morning.

"I'm staying inside," Jack insisted. Where was one sure to find beetles? Digging in the garden, naturally.

Jack occupied himself with Animal-Land. His main heroes were King Bunny and Sir Peter Mouse and Sir Ben, a frog. Naturally his heroes triumphed over any insect. From a book by Elizabeth Nesbit, Jack had discovered how things happened deep in the past. And so, that was where he placed his Animal-Land—deep in the past. That was the reason one didn't walk outside right now and see a well-armored frog striding across the garden to impale a weevil. On the other hand, Warnie's India was now, today, full of steamships and even horseless carriages!

"Look what I've made for you, Small-Piggy-Bottom," called Warnie, surprising Jack in his thoughts.

"What is it?" Jack's brows came together as he leaned toward Warnie's outstretched hand.

Warnie held out the lid to a can. On it was a layer of bright green moss. Tiny twigs were stuck upright and topped by bits of moss. Pebbles defined a path. "I brought the garden inside to you," explained Warnie.

Jack was amazed. It was very skillfully done. It was more than a garden. It was paradise in miniature. Suddenly a feeling overwhelmed him. Oh, how he wanted to possess the garden. But in a way he already possessed it. It was something else he wanted. If only he could make himself small and wander there in that green paradise. No, that wasn't it either. He had never felt such a feeling as he felt now. It was a feeling of great want, yet in itself, one of intense satisfaction.

Suddenly the feeling was gone. He was looking at a small moss-covered lid dotted with twigs and pebbles.

"Most clever, Warnie," he said, weak from the intensity of the experience.

"You seem to have little concern for what Uncle William and Poodaytabird said about me last night," complained Warnie.

"I never heard your name mentioned," Jack defended himself in surprise.

"Of course not. It's not as straight forward as that, Small-Piggy-Bottom. You see Uncle William bragged on and on how our cousins Norman and Willie have prospered in the English 'public' schools, which of course are really private schools."

"I heard him say that. So what?"

"Didn't you see the look in Poodaytabird's eyes?" Warnie prompted.

"No," Jack shook his head, bewildered.

"Well, I did, and I saw Arch-Piggy-Bottom on a ship to England!"

"No! Are you going to be sent to England?" shouted Jack. "And the rest of us are moving up into the Holywood Hills? Oh, what else can go wrong?"

The family called their new house in the Holywood Hills "Little Lea." It was three bay-windowed stories of brick, fish-scaled shingles, stucco, and dressed stone. The roof showed no fewer than five chimneys. Rooms were large and sunny. And it was poorly designed, which made it a fairy-

22

land for boys. There were isolated spaces and tunnels for no purpose whatever—except for boys to explore and inhabit. Books were stored everywhere. Poodaytabird never borrowed books; he bought them. It seemed every book he and Jack's mother wanted to read he bought. And they both dearly loved to read. Soon the boys were reading the books too. There were no restrictions.

And another great event took place. The brothers united Jack's Animal-Land with Warnie's India into a kingdom called "Boxen," generating stories and pictures furiously.

In less than a month, however, Warnie was gone. It was so suddenly after moving into Little Lea that it seemed as if Jack just looked up from his book one day and exclaimed, "Where is Warnie?"

"Off to Wynyard in Hertfordshire," replied Lizzie sourly.

"England?"

"Yes."

"Then I'm alone?"

Jack wasn't really alone in the house, for it teemed with life. There was ever-constant Lizzie as well as a housemaid, a governess, a cook, and a gardener who smelled of wine. Animals also added to the activity: Nero, a small friendly dog, various aloof cats, and even pet mice and canaries from time to time. But Jack felt alone when he squeezed into hidden recesses no one else knew about. Although his mother was home, she always seemed to be somewhere else in the house. When Poodaytabird was home, he usually read books and discussed politics in the parlor. "God forbid we get another Prime Minister like Gladstone," Poodaytabird would complain to anyone, even Jack or Nero. "What nonsense!"

Yet, Poodaytabird was not all business and politics. Once in a great while he got down on the floor and drew pictures with Jack. Another time Jack made a discovery that changed his image of Poodaytabird forever. Jack had with great relief left his father and Uncle Joseph in the parlor one evening during what was a seemingly endless discussion of politics. Later, when Jack had to retrieve a book in the room next to the parlor he heard the liveliest conversation. Several people were in the parlor now, mocking, cackling, snorting, mimicking, telling jokes, teasing, guffawing, and in general having an uproariously good time. Jack crept over to the door and peeked. It was as if he suddenly saw an elephant playing the piano. Several people were not in the parlor at all—only his father and Uncle Joseph. All the voices were coming from Poodaytabird, his walrus-mustached father!

"That's the best wheeze you've told me in a long time," chortled Uncle Joseph when Jack's father finally paused.

So that was the "wheeze" Jack's father and uncles talked about all the time! "Wheezes" were elaborate, astonishing anecdotes. Jack stayed to listen to a wheeze by Uncle Joseph, but it was a pale rendering next to his father's. From that moment on, no storyteller Jack ever heard could match his father for sheer enthusiasm and animation and mimicry. Poodaytabird's amazing talent, however, remained hidden from Jack and Warnie.

"Are all people so mysterious?" wondered Jack. "What great talent is Mother hiding from me?"

Mother was a plump, bespectacled blonde who managed the house and sat knitting or reading every evening. Her smooth, pleasant face was misleading. She was a worrier, Jack knew that. Father worried too, muttering always about financial ruin, but somehow Jack knew the muttering was no more than a release for him. Mother genuinely worried. She often disappeared with a head-ache. She was there but not there.

When Jack began his studies at home in earnest, however,

Mother became more visible. His governess Annie Harper taught him every subject except French and Latin. These were taught by his mother, who demonstrated real mastery. She also knew mathematics, Jack was told, and he asked why she did not teach him that. Her soft smile told him beyond any doubt that he would not understand such a high level of mathematics as she knew. So Jack saw another elephant playing the piano, because his mother was a greater mystery than his father. He was very proud of her after that.

The neighborhood was not without relatives to visit, but Jack usually waited for Warnie's vacations to make the rounds of their cousins with him. So, with Warnie gone most of the time, Jack began to write Boxen stories. This was not an escape where he was part of the story himself. Not at all. He had read enough books by now to know he was creating the story. The story stood alone—outside him, brimming with complicated plots and political intrigue. Not for nothing had Jack listened to Poodaytabird and his uncles talk of the real world. He knew the real world was all business and politics, but mostly politics.

On two more occasions he experienced the rush of longing he had felt when gazing at Warnie's toy garden. Once when reading *Squirrel Nutkin* he felt an overpowering longing. If only he could satisfy that hunger, yet he could not. Again he realized that the feeling of great want, in itself, was the satisfaction. Then suddenly the feeling was gone. What great mystery had he glimpsed?

Another time he was reading Longfellow—his reading varied wildly from Peter Rabbit to Milton's *Paradise Lost*. Jack liked Longfellow's poem *Saga of King Olaf* but was stunned when he ran across an unrhymed translation of an earlier poem that was little more than a footnote:

25

I heard a voice that cried,
"Balder the beautiful
Is dead, is dead!"
And through the misty air
Passed like the mournful cry
Of sunward sailing cranes.[1]

Suddenly a feeling of vast, cold northern skies overwhelmed Jack. He became sick with longing for what could only be described as something frigid and spacious and severe. Oh, how he wanted to possess what he came to think of as "Northernness." Had he once again glimpsed something beyond this world?

These glimpses into "otherness" that gave Jack sharp stabs of longing, unsatisfied, but in themselves satisfying, did not disturb him at all. He came to regard them as joy and reveled in them. Nine-year-old Jack's contentment at Little Lea seemed like it could last forever, but his world turned black indeed in 1908.

Mother Flora had no appetite and complained of fatigue and headaches. She was only forty-six. "Much too young to wear out," asserted Albert. Doctors found the problem: she was bleeding from a cancer in her stomach. Loss of blood made her tired and nauseated. As soon as possible, they performed an operation on her in the home, as was the custom for the well-to-do, but that caused another problem.

Grandfather Lewis had already been living with them for a year. Although his smoking and spitting disgusted Jack, he was nice enough, supposedly quite an important man once, a shipbuilder, they said. "Grandfather Lewis is senile now," rationalized Albert. "He makes too much noise, and he doesn't keep himself clean. He can't live in a home where someone is recuperating from major surgery." Thus

Albert justified moving Grandfather Lewis into a nursing home. Grandfather did not understand. What had he done? While Flora was recovering from her surgery, a broken Grandfather Lewis died at age seventy-six. Understandably, Albert seemed to grow much older himself.

By May, Mother was back on her feet long enough to take Jack to the seashore. She had overseen that summer excursion for years, yet it seemed the first time Jack was really aware of her presence. He studied her pleasant face for any sign of pain. Inevitably, it came. By June, pain drove her back into bed. Warnie was summoned home in July, strangely subdued, even with Jack. The outlook for Mother was grim. On the 23rd of August, Albert's birthday, she died.

"God gave us as good a woman, wife, and mother as a family ever had," Albert told the boys.

Uncle Joseph died ten days later. Grandfather, Mother, favorite uncle. All dead. How could life get worse for the Lewises?

Jack was soon to learn. . .

three

Peaks and Valleys

This time Warnie did not leave for school in England alone. Although Mother had been in the grave only days, Jack went with him. One moment Jack was running around in shorts and casual shoes, and the next moment Lizzie was dressing him in dark woolen clothes, pants that buttoned at the knees, a stiff collar, and a bowler hat. His clothes might have been made of metal for all the comfort they gave. The clothing was hot and prickly.

"They won't seem so warm in England," commented Warnie grimly.

London was not that far south, but it may as well have been on another planet. Wynyard was in the village of Watford on the lower slopes of the Chiltern Hills, remote from inviting beechwood forests to the north. Jack hated everything about Watford. The ground was sickly yellow and flinty hard. The weather was colder than any he had ever experienced. And those were the least of his complaints.

Headmaster "Oldie" was a tyrant, a smelly, thick-lipped giant. He caned the fifteen or so boys who attended classes and railed at his own teachers, even though they were ordained deacons. The lessons were so bad the boys knew they were bad. Geometry was one of the very few subjects that seemed inspired, but Jack had no interest in math anymore.

"Why didn't you tell Poodaytabird how terrible this place is?" Jack asked Warnie.

"Have you ever tried to inform Poodaytabird about any-thing?" Warnie challenged.

"He listens, but he doesn't quite hear what you say, does he?" Jack nodded understandingly.

"And suppose he wrote Oldie a letter of complaint?"

"I see. . ." Jack shuddered with the realization.

So the brothers endured the school month after month. Protected by Warnie, Jack easily slipped into the company of the other boys. Oldie's tyranny united them all. Besides learning how to cope with the complete loss of privacy, Jack discovered God again. He was appalled at first by the formal high Church of England atmosphere during services at Wynyard, but the sermons captured him. They were designed not to uplift, but to instruct. What Jack had already known in his head came to life in his heart.

He realized he really did believe in God. God was important in his life. And the fear of God was important. Lack of that fear led one straight to hell. This Jack began to appreciate all too well. Many a night he gazed out the curtainless windows of the dormitory at the moon and stars, boys snoring all around him. God was infinitely larger than the moon and stars and all of space!

"To know God is to fear him," he drilled himself in fear and trembling. Knowing God didn't seem very pleasant.

After a year Warnie moved on to Malvern, a school for older boys many miles away, closer to Bristol than London. As the second year started at Wynyard Jack knew his low opinion of the school was shared by many outside the school. The Wynyard School that Poodaytabird had checked out so carefully five years before was nearly dead. Jack was one of only five students! After another year at Wynyard, even Albert had to admit Wynyard was doing Jack, now eleven, more harm than good. By July of 1910, Jack was home at Little Lea, certain that he would never return to Wynyard.

He plunged into Boxen. Now he had time to write. When Warnie came home, he read some of Jack's most recent writing about the 'Jah of India and King Bunny of Animal-Land:

> *Night was falling on the Bosphorus as the town guardsman sighted a small but tidy schooner tacking up to Fortressa. For'ad stood a young Tracity Chessary Pawn and at the tiller a sturdy thickset knight stolidly smoking his pipe. With a little deft maneuvering he brought her up a secluded rocky creek and dropped anchor about 200 yards from the shingle. He called the assistant of the Pawn to lower his solitary boat, which soon was lying under the schooner's counter, and several vigorous strokes sent him to the beach. Mooring the boat he stepped out and in the dusk descried two tall athletic figures walking along a short distance away.*
> *"Why! Your majesties!"*
> *They turned. "Macgoullah."*
> *"At your service. What are you doing here?"*
> *"Oh," said the 'Jah, "Learning Turkish."*
> *"Alone?" inquired the knight.*
> *"No. Big's here," answered Bunny.*
> *"At the inn?"*
> *"Yes."*
> *The three friends walked together to the postern gate, where the guard admitted them for a small fee. A few hundred yards brought them to the inn. Through the door into the Inner room Macgoullah caught sight of a stout frog in evening dress. . .[1]*

Warnie looked up. "Did you copy this from a novel?"

"I wrote it myself," declared Jack firmly.

"Rather too many adjectives," Warnie criticized, but he seemed stunned.

For six months Jack remained at Little Lea halfheartedly attending a nearby school while Albert made arrangements for him to be taken in at Cherbourg Preparatory School, next to Warnie's Malvern School. In January, Jack was off to England again with Warnie.

Warnie's face quickly donned the smuggest look Jack had ever seen. Now fifteen, Warnie studied his manicured nails. "This time, Jack, I believe at twelve you're old enough to enjoy England."

And Jack did enjoy England. Now when he and Warnie sailed the Irish Channel from Belfast to Liverpool, they didn't breathlessly catch the first train south. No, they found a pleasant cafe and puffed cigarettes and read books for several hours. Then they leisurely returned to Malvern, preferably on the slowest train in England.

Now that the teachers were competent and Jack was challenged, school pleased him. In spite of his intense dislike for competitive sports, he got along with the other twenty or so boys. He even liked the surroundings, the soft green hills to the west and the low blue plain of the Severn River to the east.

The matron who looked after the boys made his days at Cherbourg even more pleasant. She was very kind, very popular, and she loved to discuss religion. But hers was not the cut-and-dried Christianity of the Church of England. She had moved beyond that. She discussed theosophy and spiritualism. She told the boys of a spirit world—not necessarily Christian—waiting beyond the material world. The challenge, she purported, was to communicate with that world.

31

Jack's strong imagination was fertile soil for the words of his matron, and he trusted her. He began to long for that hidden world about which his matron talked.

During that time, Jack was also reading the classics in Latin and Greek. All these pagan writers discussed religion. Jack realized that ideas about religion were very old and assumed many forms. Was not one about as right as the other? Even more damning was the thought that religion had simply grown out of a fear of death. Might it be no more than a story to ease one's fears?

A couplet from Lucretius in Latin chilled Jack as he translated it:

> Had God designed the world, it would not be
> A world so frail and faulty as we see.

Jack discerned that many of his teachers embraced the ideas he was encountering in the classics and noticed that most of his fellow students were following the teachers, moving beyond mere disinterest to a complete shedding of their religion. They perceived religion as a very tiresome duty and the fear of God as a most unpleasant attitude. Eventually Jack realized not only did he no longer fear God, he did not believe in God at all. Spirits might be beyond the material world, but not the demanding God of the Bible. He felt free.

"It really is time to move on to more substantial things," he cajoled his companions, and no one disagreed.

Despite not experiencing—and actually forgetting—his "otherness" for several years, Jack found it again. Then, by pure accident, one day he saw in a magazine the words *Siegfried* and the *Twilight of the Gods*. Suddenly a feeling of vast, cold northern skies overwhelmed him again. He became sick with longing for something cold and spacious and severe: his old "Northernness." Again, the unfulfilled desire became satisfaction in itself and seemed a glimpse into another world. "Not the simple-minded sterile spirit world of the matron," he told himself, "but something grand."

Jack learned that *Siegfried and the Twilight of the Gods* was an opera composed by the German Richard Wagner and forthwith changed his opinion that operas were simply overweight men and women screaming unintelligibly in German and Italian. Soon he was playing Wagner's operas on a phonograph, immersed in *Rhinegold* and then the Ring Trilogy itself. The music added yet another dimension to Jack's fondness for "Northernness." The yearnings of his heart, however, were focused on those occasional glimpses into unutterable joy.

The late summer of 1913 brought great changes again to the Lewis brothers. "I've decided to join Field Marshall Kitchener," Warnie told Jack, wearing an expression he had now cultivated from mere smugness into absolute British superiority.

Kitchener was a great military hero, subduing the heathens in Sudan and keeping order in Warnie's beloved India. So Warnie had decided to make the army a career. There was only one way to launch a successful career in the army: one had to graduate from Sandhurst, England's great military academy. First things first, however; one had to pass a very difficult entrance examination to gain the privilege of attending Sandhurst.

"I'll prepare myself most diligently," Warnie boasted.

"What nonsense! Old Kirk will prepare you for the exam right proper," Albert announced, referring to his own tutor, W. T. Kirkpatrick, who lived in Great Bookham, south of London.

Jack's great change came when he moved on to Malvern

School. How he had anticipated it! During frequent visits at Malvern School, he, along with the other Cherbourg boys, had been entranced at listening to the older boys. They represented the next necessary step to world power and glory. Warnie, an enthusiastic competitor at sports, had stood out there, so Jack had been treated with respect on his visits.

But now Warnie was gone. From Jack's first day, Malvern was misery and torment. Jack had no quality of his own that the older boys respected. There was no doubt about this because with great relish they told him. He was not only no good at sports, he was a coward who avoided them. Neither was he particularly good looking; in fact, he looked either hangdog or downright insolent. Furthermore, his personality was a pitiful sham; he was only a mimic. His chance to eventually become a "Blood," a member of the ruling class of students, was nonexistent. Beyond the verbal abuse was floggings. Jack himself was flogged for missing an event because a Blood had lied to him. And then there was the fact that younger boys were in constant servitude to the Bloods.

The humiliation was eased for Jack by the school library and one teacher. Younger boys were safe from Bloods only in the library. So Jack both found refuge and indulged his voracious reading habits there. Who knows how many hundreds of books he had read by the age of fifteen? And he knew, if no one else did, that he retained what he read: word for word.

The teacher who inspired him was nicknamed Smewgy. Smewgy taught Classics and English. He could read poetry with the subtlety of a Shakespearean actor. And more, he knew his subjects. He was neither familiar nor unfriendly. He quipped no cheap humor, only pungent comments.

"Smewgy is both a perfect teacher and a perfect gentleman," gushed Jack.

The return home for winter vacation break yielded no relief for Jack. Little Lea became its own battleground. Jack's descriptions of Malvern's horrors and his pleas for Albert to remove him roused Warnie to defend his alma mater. For the first time, the brothers were really hostile to each other. Aside from the fraternal strife, Albert was haranguing Warnie.

"Old Kirk has written me that you are almost hopeless as a pupil, Warren."

"Perhaps I know a bit more than the old boy realizes," retorted Warnie defiantly.

"What nonsense!" ranted Albert.

Normally Jack could not have been whipped into visiting a neighbor, Arthur Greeves, who was Warnie's age, but now Arthur was sick and Jack was glad for any excuse to get out of Little Lea for a while. Arthur had tried to make friends in the past, but the brothers would allow no one inside their circle. Besides that, Arthur, tall and thin, blonde and rosy-cheeked, was a hypochondriac and very spoiled. Now as Jack stood by Arthur's bedside just enjoying being away from Little Lea, he spotted on the nightstand a book he had just read himself. *Myths of the Norseman* was the epitome of "Northernness"!

"I say, do you like that?" probed Jack cautiously.

"Do you?" returned Arthur in astonishment.

Soon they were sharing exact experiences of longing and indescribable stabs of joy. Their mutual love of "Northernness" seemed too good to be true. Arthur even loved books as much as Jack. Not just their substance, but their binding, their print, their page margins, their paper weight, their totality! Arthur's every fault was instantly invisible.

Jack had found a soul-mate. Jack and Arthur planned to write each other. Sharing their "Northernness" and love of books would make Malvern tolerable for Jack.

Almost miraculously, the strife among the Lewises that had ushered in the new year of 1914 was virtually forgotten by the end of January. Besides being buoyed by shared joys with his new-found friend Arthur, Jack was elated by Albert's promise that he would not only take him out of Malvern but would send him to W. T. Kirkpatrick to be privately tutored.

Perhaps the most incredible development was Warnie's superior performance on the Sandhurst entrance exam. Albert was openly jubilant. "Warnie, you've placed twenty-first out of over 200 candidates. You've confounded me and Old Kirk. You're being accepted as one of twenty-five 'prize cadets'!"

Jack survived the few remaining months of Malvern by indulging his Northernness. Inspired by Norse mythology, he wrote a play in classical Greek poetry which he titled, *Loki Bound*. Jack, more and more sure his first calling was poetry, began to collect his lyrical poems in a volume he called *Metrical Meditations of a Cod*. He wrote a poem for Smewgy's class that seemed a farewell:

> *Of the host whom I named*
> *As friends, ye alone,*
> *Dear few! were ashamed*
> *In troubles unknown*
> *To leave me deserted, but boldly ye*
> *cherished my cause as your own. . .*[2]

In August of 1914, when the Great War broke out in Europe, Warnie's honored status at Sandhurst turned into what seemed to Albert a death sentence. Warnie was going to be rushed through training and sent to France to fight the Germans.

Jack left for Great Bookham, the village in Surrey, south of London, where he would live with his tutor, W.T. Kirkpatrick. Warnie had told Jack that Surrey was developed and populated, but from the train Jack saw only raw creeks and woods thick enough to be called a forest.

W.T. Kirkpatrick, white-haired and mustached, met him at the station. The older man was very tall and so thin that even his face seemed exposed muscles. His grip confirmed his wiry nature. He was every inch "Old Kirk."

As they walked from the station Jack said breezily, "I was surprised at the scenery. Surrey is wilder than I expected."

"What do you mean by 'wild'? And what basis do you have for your expectations? Maps? Perhaps some publications on the flora and fauna of Surrey?"

Jack stared at Kirkpatrick. The man was serious. "No, sir, I have no maps or publications. I was merely making conversation," replied Jack dubiously.

"Why would you do that?" demanded W. T. Kirkpatrick. "Tell me, what are your reasons?"

Jack fended off question after question all the way to Kirkpatrick's house. His anger cooled as he realized the incessant questions were not intended to be harassment or judgment or conversation or joking. The process was simply Kirkpatrick's way of knowing, as well as of making Jack realize he had used "wild" with no real definition in mind. Jack became very fond of W.T. Kirkpatrick, soon thinking of him as "Kirk."

Kirk, as unique as Smewgy, was Jack's second great teacher. Whereas Smewgy's strength was in grammar and rhetoric, Kirk's strength was in dialectics, or discovering the truth through questioning dialogue. Jack guarded every statement now. He could have withdrawn, but he did not. Kirk was too sincere and too kind for Jack to respond in such a manner. Jack, an atheist now himself, was not bothered at all to find out Kirk was an atheist. Kirk was the only kind of atheist who mattered. He had reasoned it out, looking at every side of the cosmic issue.

Oddly, Kirk honored the Lord's Day and started Jack on Homer the next day. He simply read a few opening lines out of the *Iliad* and left Jack on his own. Jack floundered at first but quickly began to crave such independence. After a few days, he felt he was in paradise. He ate breakfast, prepared by kind Mrs. Kirkpatrick, at eight o'clock, then was at his desk at nine-fifteen studying or writing until one o'clock with a small tea break at eleven. After lunch he took a bracing walk. At four o'clock he returned for afternoon tea, then studied at his desk until seven. After dinner was time for discussions with Kirk or light reading or writing letters. At eleven o'clock he was in bed. Bed was delicious. The volume of work he was doing was astonishing. He had never been happier.

When Warnie got a leave from the Great War in France in early 1915, he stopped by Surrey to join Jack on a trip home to Little Lea. Albert looked at both sons differently now. Warnie was a grown man of almost twenty, a combat veteran. And Albert looked at sixteen-year-old Jack differently. Was it pride? Or was it disappointment?

"Did Kirk give you a report on me?" Jack investigated.

"So he did," revealed Albert. "Says you have mature and original literary judgment. Says you know first-rate work unerringly and can discern why it is first-rate."

So just as Albert and Warnie had focused on Sandhurst for a military career, now Albert and Jack began to consider the great choice any serious English scholar had to make: Oxford University or Cambridge University. Because Jack disliked science and mathematics, Cambridge, considered more in league with hard-boiled science than Oxford, was eliminated. From then on, Kirk was to prepare Jack with the eventual goal of passing the entrance exams at Oxford.

By no means did Jack abandon Arthur or his love of books. In early 1916, when he discovered *Phantastes* by George MacDonald, he whooped, "I must write Arthur!"

To Arthur he poured out his happiness over finding George MacDonald. Another author to add to their circle! Not since *The Well at the World's End* by William Morris had Jack enjoyed a book so much. He was sure once Arthur followed the hero Anodos along the little stream to the fairy wood like he had, Arthur would agree MacDonald was superb. Jack mentioned the terrible ash tree and how the shadow of its gnarled, knotted hand falls upon the book Anodos is reading, and other scenes in *Phantastes* that had so forcefully struck him. Later that same year Jack wrote Arthur about the "Golden Key," a remarkable short story by George MacDonald. "What would I do without Arthur to confide in?" he exulted. What a joy to have such a close friend!

Life was wonderful for Jack. Every waking hour was filled with reading and writing, but finally came the time for accounting. In December he took the entrance examination at Oxford. Although the great spired University was deep in the grip of winter and half shut down by the war, the exam was administered for several days in the Hall of Oriel College. The Hall, with its hammer-beam roof, was so cold Jack never removed his overcoat or his left glove.

Afterwards he told Kirk, "There were no questions on the Latin and Greek authors I know best. I probably did fine on a question about Samuel Johnson, but I must admit I was stymied by a question on an esoteric poem by the German author, Goethe. . ."

"Is that so?" queried Kirk, pale as a ghost.

When Jack arrived at Little Lea on winter break, he found that Kirk had written Albert that he was beside himself with worry because Jack had probably failed. Albert was very depressed. Not even Jack's reminders of how pessimistic Kirk had been about Warnie's chances with the Sandhurst exam could cheer Albert up. "What nonsense," he would mutter.

The house seemed like a great empty barn now with only Albert, a housekeeper, and an aloof new dog, Tim. Albert waited with dread for the letter from Oxford. On December 13, it came.

Jack opened the letter, then looked at Albert with his best deadpan face. "It seems I've received a scholarship to University College at Oxford University. . ."

Inside, Jack was rapturous. Although Percy Shelley had studied at "Univ" until they had thrown him out for being an atheist, they were more tolerant now to atheistic poets— like Jack. In April 1917, Jack began his studies at Oxford in spite of failing an additional test, called "Responsions," because of his inept mathematics. England was in no mood to quibble. Jack could take the test again—after the war. One month later he began Officer Training.

Since his mother had died in 1908, Jack's life had been peak and valley. Up and down. Down and up. The misery of Wynyard. The joy of Cherbourg. The misery of Malvern. The joy of studying with Kirk. And now this ultimate misery, this abomination: war. *Will this be the last valley? Will there be another peak?*

"I don't think so," reflected Jack aloud, slumped against the sandbags of the trench. Fondly remembering Kirk's favorite expression, he quirked a wobbly grin and added, "And I think my opinion is based on sufficient knowledge." The trench was silent. Death had finally claimed the poor Irish enlisted man who had been wounded by the exploding shell.

"Lieutenant Lewis?"

"Yes, sir!" Jack snapped to attention. To see the Major in the front trench was rare.

The Major took him aside. "Bit of news, Lewis. Jerries have broken through our front lines to the north. Good old Somerset has to hit them from the side. Round up your men. Say good-bye to the trenches."

So there it is, thought Jack. The bell tolled for him at last. Death. . .

four

"Lieutenant Lewis, we can't move to the north in the front-line trench," instructed the Major. "That would be too slow. We've got to move back through the communication trenches, then get out into the open."

The Somerset Light Infantry wormed its way back several miles through the communication trenches. Jack learned the German Sixth Army had overrun the Portuguese troops to the north. The only good news was that there was no mustard gas. The Germans weren't about to saturate an area with gas that they expected to occupy themselves in a few hours. If there was a sudden onset of cold weather, the garlicky-smelling mustard gas could linger for days. No, the Germans had simply crushed the Portuguese with artillery, trench mortars, hand grenades, machine guns, and tanks.

"Why are we marching at night?" questioned Thorne. "Aren't we miles and miles from the krauts?"

"Their spotter planes will see us," explained Sergeant Ayres.

"This way we'll surprise the Germans," added Jack sarcastically. "They would never expect us to counterattack."

"You'd better take this," murmured Thorne, handing Jack his bound copy of *The Memoirs of Benvenuto Cellini*. His eyes told Jack he was certain he was going to die.

The Somerset, weighed down with supplies, waited for

dusk before leaving the rear trenches. Walking across open ground, the men felt strangely naked. For weeks in the trenches, Jack had learned to ignore the brilliant flares called Very Lights. Now he was acutely aware of them again. They lit up the sky many miles to the north where the Germans were busy killing.

As dawn neared they found some rear trenches and slept. At dusk they ate and marched again. In the distance, artillery shells screamed. Presumably, the shells were flying east as well as west. Occasionally Jack heard the knock-knock-knock of machine gun fire. Minutes before dawn he smelled smoke.

"From barges in the La Bassee canal," offered someone.

Jack learned that the barges had been set afire on the orders of some jittery British general to prevent the Germans from using them. The Germans, however, had not gotten that far. If war weren't so hideous, thought Jack, it might be amusing at times. Incredibly, the bridge across the canal had been left standing.

"I'm ready for some shuteye," said Thorne just ahead of him. "Where is the trench?"

"No trench here, sir," said Sergeant Ayres. "We'll sleep in funkholes. Close to the hedges."

"Hedges? What hedges?" slurred Thorne in a tired voice.

Dawn revealed hedges all over the countryside. The Somerset began scraping shallow holes as close as possible to the hedges. The holes would be just deep enough to keep their noses below shrapnel from exploding shells. The men began to grumble as they chopped through hedge roots, then discovered the ground was sticky clay only six inches below loamy soil. So they dug farther down into the muck, then covered the mess with topsoil so the clay would not stick to their clothing and gear. In full light, Jack looked around at the landscape. Cottages, gardens, and hedges. Even trees. This part of France wasn't like No Man's Land.

"Yet," he croaked as he drifted into sleep.

They arose that evening to eat tins of pork and beans and bully beef. Hardtack and plum jam did not compensate for the huge containers of hot stew they had downed in the trenches. Some soldiers of the Somerset were now assigned positions and stayed as the rest moved on to the north. Jack's battalion had the northernmost position. He trudged on, remembering the mouse in March. The shelling had been awful, three a minute all day. The poor shivering mite had actually wanted to run to him for comfort. Was it a sign? Jack had dearly loved mice all his life. But how could he believe such a thing? From whom was the sign? The devil?

"Better dig in, sir," commanded Sergeant Ayres.

"Dig in?" Jack was startled. He had actually slept while marching. "Of course."

Out of his battalion, Jack's platoon was nearly the last to be stationed to the north. He was on a rise called Mount Berenchon, near the village of Lillers. He and his platoon were a good twenty or so miles from where they had left the front lines.

At dawn on April 15, 1918, Jack could see the war right in front of him. Planes flimsy as dragonflies, scouting armies, and occasionally dropping bombs. Tanks belching smoke. Shellbursts spraying dirt. He was grateful that his platoon was well behind the fighting. No trench mortars this far back. How he hated that Roman candle "poof!" of the mortars! Then the shell dropped right into a man's funkhole. And the grenades, the potato-mashers. They made no sound at all until they exploded. If one hit a man, he never heard anything. It was too late. His life ended on a heartbeat.

"The krauts are a hundred deep," estimated Sergeant Ayres, who now stood up.

Jack stood up too. Yes, Ayres was right. The German forces stretched to the horizon. Several divisions must have massed against the First British Army between Bethune and Armentieres. The Germans were getting closer too. Jack could actually watch them. The gallant Somerset were going to be annihilated. . .

"What was that?" someone screamed.

Jack's mind was spinning. Was he lying on his back? He wasn't sure. He couldn't see anything. He had been hit, probably. He didn't seem to be breathing, but he could hear voices. He had to be alive. No, he wasn't breathing. He was alive but dying. His thoughts were dying embers. He felt nothing. No regret. No sorrow. Nothing. It was over.

Or was he dreaming? The sounds of war still popped and cracked. His knees and palms hurt from sharp stones. Somehow he was on his hands and knees. His left arm hurt. Chest too. He began crawling. Perhaps he was not dead. He was alive. But was he dying? Was he one of those poor crushed men who crawl about for a while like a smashed roach? Was this the last grim joke of a Godless universe? He got to crawl like a stepped-on insect for a while, then die. Sharp pain stabbed him as he collapsed.

"Never mind the sergeant!" someone barked. "He's dead."

What seemed ages later, Jack heard muted voices, but he felt nothing. Saw nothing. So something was beyond death after all. Something dark and muted and slightly insane. It was the "dreary miasma" of the Pagan Hell, the Sheol of the Jews. The soul wandered in a stupor for eternity. Was this the edict of a merciless God?

"It's dressed, doctor," announced a woman's voice. Was

Jack alive? He tried to open his eyes. Yes, he saw light! "Can you hear me, Lieutenant?" prodded the woman's voice. "You got a blighty."

A blighty! Jack's mind grappled with the information. A bad wound, but not a fatal one. Bad enough to get a man sent to the hospital for a while. Maybe bad enough to get him sent back to England! Jack felt his heart thumping with joy. "You're at Liverpool Merchants Mobile Hospital in Etaples, Lieutenant," supplied the voice.

Etaples. That was on the coast of France. How long had he been unconscious? Something jolted him. Some hard thing was shoved roughly underneath his hips. He was on his back. The bedpan allowed him to figure that out.

Sometime later, when his sight returned, he floated in a sea of white. Fans were above on a high ceiling. Beds stretched as far as he could see. And in the beds were bandage-wrapped men. "What day is it?" Jack asked the nurse who finally appeared. When he had asked the men around him, he had gotten no answer. Apparently they were unconscious.

"April 16, Lieutenant."

"Just one day?" his forehead wrinkled.

She looked at his chart. "Yes, sir. You were wounded yesterday."

"What about the others? Sergeant Ayres and Laurence Johnson and. . ."

"I don't know, sir. I only see the soldiers who are brought here. I never know anything about the battlefield. I'm very sorry."

"You're very lucky," Jack corrected, nodding.

The next day Jack wrote a letter to his father. Writing was difficult both because he was sore and heavily bandaged and because of its recipient. Every word had to be weighed with careful consideration. If Jack minimized his wounds, Poodaytabird might be frantic because the wound was not bad enough to get him sent home. If he exaggerated the wounds, however, Poodaytabird might be frantic with worry. Now that Jack thought about it, he became rather angry. He had wired his father to visit in him in Bristol before he was shipped out to France, and his father had not understood his wire at all. Either that or his father was still angry because Jack had spent most of his last leave with Paddy Moore in Bristol. Actually, Jack didn't know much about his wounds, only that his left arm was bandaged against his side, and his left hand hurt. Finally deciding that no matter what he wrote his father would make a thorough mess of it, he wrote that he had a flesh wound in his left arm.

That day Jack finally saw a doctor. "Do I have a blighty or not?" he asked bluntly.

"Yes, Lieutenant. You do indeed. You have shrapnel in your hand. That is minor. You have a tiny bit behind the knee in your left leg. That is minor. You have a chunk or two that went in under your left armpit. They are somewhere in your chest. They are not minor."

"I see. What about the others in my platoon?"

"Your battalion took heavy losses, I'm afraid."

"Sergeant Ayres and Laurence Johnson?" Jack prompted.

"I have no way of knowing." The doctor edged away.

Not until a soldier came in who was wounded the day after Jack was did Jack found out how terribly the battalion had been mauled by the Germans. The shell that had hit Jack had been a fluke, maybe from their own artillery. Sergeant Ayres was dead, perhaps hit by the same shell that had felled Jack. He'd been Jack's protector to the very end.

Laurence Johnson was dead too. Jack's friend. After Jack

heard that, he closed his mind and stopped listening. Once again he had lost those who had meant the most to him. He couldn't bring himself to ask about Thorne.

He wrote letters to the living to take his mind off the dead. He read Anthony Trollope and Sir Walter Scott. He wrote poetry about Oxford, the war, and "spirit":

> *It is well that there are palaces of peace*
> *And discipline and dreaming and desire,*
> *Lest we forget our heritage and cease*
> *The Spirit's work—to hunger and aspire:*
> *Lest we forget that we were born divine,*
> *Now tangled in red battle's animal net,*
> *Murder the work and lust the anodyne,*
> *Pains of the beast 'gainst bestial solace set.*
> *But this shall never be: to us remains*
> *One city that has nothing of the beast,*
> *That was not built for gross, material gains,*
> *Sharp, wolfish power or empire's glutted feast.*
> *We are not wholly brute. To us remains*
> *A clean, sweet city. . .[1]*

Jack rather shocked himself by what he had written. He had certainly hinted at the existence of God. Jack's tiny chip of some unthinking universal spirit had grown! He argued with himself until he beat down his feeling of a Supreme Thinking Being. Surely he had written the poem for Arthur's sake. After all, Arthur was the one who believed man was "born divine." And Jack didn't hold that against him.

One day Warnie burst into the ward. "You look like a mummy!"

"What!" exclaimed Jack in mock surprise. "I didn't know you supply officers got this close to the front lines."

"Only to gawk at shrapnel in small-piggy-bottoms!"

"You look like you've run a marathon," teased Jack, noting Warnie's salt-stained shirt.

"I pedaled a bicycle all the way from my post. Fifty miles, old boy. Poodaytabird wrote me about your wounds. How are you?"

"Got a blighty for sure, Warnie. Shrapnel lodged in my pigeon chest near faint heart. Doctor says he will leave the metal there. No harm will come from it, I suppose," Jack shrugged.

Warnie betrayed some agitation at how well Jack was doing. Jack, instead of being petulant about it, enjoyed that irony very much. It was just the kind of ironic humor he thought very amusing. Their hostility over Malvern had apparently dissolved, and it almost seemed they would suddenly get on the floor and invent Boxen stories together. Jack's spirit lifted from Warnie's visit, and he was amused to think Warnie, now a captain no less, slightly overweight and probably drinking and smoking every idle hour, had to pedal back fifty miles to his post.

Progress in Jack's first days was very slow. Just being able to sleep on his right side after sleeping on his back for a month seemed a great triumph.

Near the end of May the hospital was shelled. Jack, in bed and bandaged as tight as a repulsive pupae in a cocoon, was more terrified now than he had been in the trenches. Oh, would the grim ironies ever end?

"I can't hide and I can't run," he complained to a nurse, expecting no answer.

Days later Jack was transported across the English Channel to England. On the ship Jack thrilled to the salt air and chopping sea. Later, from the window of the train, England was a feast. After the drab, cratered no-man's-land and the blanched hospital, England glowed a bright jolly green he had never seen before. Streams sparkled like blue diamonds. Hedges glinted silver. Distant fields of buttercups shimmered as plains of pure gold.

His hospital in London was a real palace: Endsleigh Palace in Endsleigh Gardens. The rooms were private and the beds large. Jack, now sitting up and feeling very fortunate, was exchanging letters with Arthur and admitting that the thrills he had felt from "otherness" were indeed contacts with some spirit world. Far from being the spirit realm of some Great Benevolent Creator of the material world, however, the spirit world he imagined was the sworn enemy of the material world.

"So perhaps Laurence Johnson was right," Jack needled himself. "Maybe I am thinking like the mad genius William Blake." Blake's impenetrable prophecies made him shudder.

Jack asked Arthur if he could return a manuscript with some of his early poems. He was planning to assemble a book of his poems and submit it for publication. He had been writing poetry all along. It seemed his calling. What wasn't on paper was in his head. His theme was that nature was wholly diabolical. If God existed at all, He was outside the cosmos and even disapproved of it. The obvious conclusion was that nature was a creation of a very powerful devil. Men had to struggle against the devil, unaided by an indifferent God. The slaughter of war only strengthened Jack's convictions. He wasn't going to try to publish some monotonous manuscript all in one kind of meter either. His theme would be offered in an interesting variety of meters.

The London bookshops accelerated Jack's recovery. By mid-June he was walking short distances. How else could he get to the books? He bought and read as many books as he could afford. He also visited Kirk one Sunday in Great

Bookham, surprising the old man in his garden among the cabbages. Although Kirk greeted him warmly, Jack was very pleased he received no special treatment.

"I think your opinion is based on insufficient knowledge, Clive," Kirk would say again and again as they spoke in dialectics. Kirk was the only person in the world who called Jack "Clive."

But time began to wear Jack down. He wasn't quite as hale and hearty as he pretended. He wished he could see Warnie or Arthur or even his father. He had been on the mend for over two months and in London nearly one month now, but still his father had not visited him. Jack was surprised at how much that hurt. Toward the end of one letter to his father he poured out his pain:

> *I know that you will come and see me. . .I was never before so eager to cling to every bit of our old home life and to see you. I know I have often been far from what I should be in my relation to you, and have undervalued (your) affection and generosity. . .But, please God, I shall do better in the future. Come and see me, I am homesick, that is the long and short of it. . .*[2]

Still Albert did not come!

A letter from Arthur hinted that Albert was drinking heavily. Perhaps he was. Two sons in France in a war that was killing men by the millions could do that to a man who lived alone and brooded, and Albert was phobic anyway about things not in his routine. He had never been able to stay with Flora and the boys in the summers at the seashore. Within minutes he would be pulling out his pocket watch, nerves a-jangle, looking like he was on the verge of hysteria.

51

One person who did seem to care enough about Jack to visit him without fail in London was Paddy Moore's mother. Paddy was dead. All five of the boys who had visited Mrs. Moore in the Oxford Officer Training days were dead— except Jack.

"Oh, why can't the British and Americans finish off the Germans?" lamented Mrs. Moore, quickly adding, "not that you'll have to go back to France, dear boy."

Jack, finally ready for the next step in rehabilitation, was scheduled to be moved to a "convalescent home." After requesting one in Ireland and being told they were few in number and already crowded, he asked for one where he knew he would have at least one faithful friend. Thus, in July he was convalescing in Bristol, the city where Mrs. Moore lived.

The "convalescent home" was a thirteenth-century castle, much altered over hundreds of years. Wooded surroundings offered solitary walks interrupted occasionally by a bolting deer. Thankfully, Jack enjoyed the walks very much now, for, much to his disappointment, the library in the castle was kept locked. Other convalescing soldiers gave Jack ample evidence, however, for that restriction. The men seemed ignorant idlers, playing billiards and killing time. Jack found a small writing room where he could escape the whistling and chatter to read and write. He still corresponded with his father, consistently inviting him to visit. Albert still remained friendly and caring in his letters but would not visit. Jack withdrew more and more from him. Jack's only constant visitor was Mrs. Moore.

"A scholar the likes of you, dear boy, with no library," she would say while visiting. "You're starved for reading. Here's a trifle from Maureen."

One day Jack was more pleased than ever with her visit.

"Why, it's *The Princess and the Goblin* by George Mac-Donald! One of his 'Curdie' books."

"Maureen reads many fairy tales," excused Mrs. Moore.

"Oh, this is of most excellent taste! It will lead the child into poetry and fantasy, not the cheap, twaddling novels of so many modern readers."

Jack found this "Curdie" story a delight. It was the best kind of fantasy, a story pulled along by the thrill of an adventure, yet bursting with profound meanings. In one part, the sleeping boy Curdie dreams he is waking up, but waking up is only a dream. To Jack this meant a person on a spiritual journey could imagine he had transformed himself, yet be merely indulging in the pleasure of the idea of changing, and not changing at all. The real work remained to be done.

"The significance of that is terrifying," he admitted to himself, yet he craved the writings of MacDonald. To think that Mrs. Moore should bring him such pleasure. How his spirits would collapse without her!

Mrs. Janie Moore appeared too young to be the mother of Paddy. A solidly built blond with smooth milky skin, her strong jaw was softened by lively eyes and bubbling energy. Her kindness was overwhelming, yet not suffocating. When Jack let the war and his father's inexplicable neglect poison his thoughts, she was the perfect antidote. To think Jack had promised Paddy to look after his mother; in fact, she looked after Jack.

"Dear boy, I lost my mother too," she confided to Jack. "It's a pain like no other. I was a mere schoolgirl in Lincoln. It seems like yesterday."

"It *was* yesterday," declared Jack, flattering her, "but whereas I was sent to school, you were brought back from school." Jack was already quite knowledgeable about Mrs.

Moore's life.

"Yes, my father had a large family of very young children. As a man of God, he had a lot of counsel but little money, you can be sure of that. Someone had to be his housekeeper. I was the oldest of the three girls. . ."

Jack interrupted her proudly, "Well, that's surely why you are such a wonderful mother."

five

J ack was proud of Mrs. Janie Moore. She had weathered a very trying life, yet never surrendered her generosity and good cheer. Her father, Reverend William Askins, was a very hard man. Her sister Edie and her brother Rob, both of whom lived in Bristol too, confirmed that. Janie had helped raise the children until her own marriage. She was a prize: industrious, reliable, beautiful. She had married "well." Mister Courtenay Moore was not only an engineer, but also a gentleman related to Lord Drogheda, a peerage from King Charles the Second. Yet, Courtenay Moore was a brute. After Maureen was born, Mrs. Moore summoned the courage to take the two children and leave her husband. Of course, divorce in Ireland was impossible. . .

"You know, Jack, we must have a party for all your poor comrades at the home," Mrs. Moore proposed during a visit.

"If you wish," Jack conceded with little enthusiasm.

The idea was so typical of Mrs. Moore. Her greatest quality was hospitality. Jack, who tried to exclude uninteresting people from his circle, knew somehow Mrs. Moore was much more correct to include one and all. She was his mentor in all social things, including religion. In spite of being the daughter of a clergyman she was very practical about religion. Yes, religion was desirable—how else could society keep some men from behaving like beasts?—but it should not be allowed to interfere with modern thinking.

"Suffer it as a pleasant social duty," advised Mrs. Moore.

Jack continued to compile his poetry. He now had the book organized into three parts: "The Prison House," "Hesitation," and "Escape." He was pragmatic, stating ahead of time that he would send it to all the large publishers. Mrs. Moore cheered him on. Even if all the publishers rejected his proposal, he would at least have gained some professional critiques of his poems and have them nicely typewritten and preserved. As August 1918 approached, no publisher had accepted his book proposal, now titled *Spirits in Prison: A cycle of lyrical poems,* but he had a larger problem.

"August is the month I'm rumored to return to France, Mother," he confided to Mrs. Moore.

"But your shortness of breath from the shrapnel. Surely they can't send you back just yet."

"You don't know as I do how illogical the army is," he wanted to protest. . .

Yet when Mrs. Moore next came to visit him, Jack yelped, "You were right all along!"

The doctors had pronounced him not ready to return to the fighting yet. Now he had only his *Spirits in Prison* to fret over. He had written Arthur that he was inserting new pieces and deleting old ones, so much so that he had finally begun to doubt his judgment. Perhaps he had tinkered with it too much. "Perhaps I only made it worse. . ." he penned to Arthur.

And then to his amazement the manuscript was accepted by William Heinemann in London. So alienated was Jack from his father, that only now—and for the first time—did he write him about the book of poetry. Homebound Albert answered enthusiastically, helpfully pointing out that *Spirits in Prison* was a title already in use. Jack duly decided to change the title to *Spirits in Bondage*. When Albert quoted Scripture and invoked Christ's blessing, however, Jack was repulsed. The constant invitations to his father to come and visit had humiliated Jack. No excuse he could think of was sufficient for a delay of four months. As a result, his requests for Albert to visit, heartfelt in May, turned sarcastic by September.

To Mrs. Moore he admitted, "My longing for Little Lea is almost dead."

"That's sad. But you have a home here."

Jack, citing the army as his reason for using a pen name, had his book published under "Clive Hamilton" to honor the memory of his mother. When he went back to his regiment—and the day to return was getting closer, he did not want to be known as "that starry-eyed poet" by every ignorant lout that hated the finer things. In October he was posted to a depot at Eastbourne in Sussex. Nightmares of war blighted his sleep again.

Eastbourne was on the coast directly across the channel from France. "It doesn't take a genius to figure out where I will be moved next," he fretted to Mrs. Moore.

During the day he read classics, reminding himself that the war would end and Oxford would be his next stop. "I forgot less than I had feared," he eagerly revealed to Mrs. Moore. "The rhythms of the languages have returned. It should not be too long before I can compose competently too."

"We must be ready for Oxford," replied Mrs. Moore.

"By all means," affirmed Jack.

Although he had no enthusiasm to write his father, he wrote nonetheless, telling himself it was one way to keep a diary—his father saved everything in that barn of a house. Boldly he wrote his father that Mrs. Moore and her daughter

Maureen were there to comfort him. What cad could possibly think anything was uncouth in such an arrangement? Would a lady do anything improper in the company of her daughter? Mrs. Moore wrote his father too, explaining the vows Jack and Paddy had exchanged before leaving for France. Jack was now her son too.

About nine o'clock in the evening of November 10, 1918, every siren in Eastbourne screamed. Searchlights swept the sky. Officers ran into the parade ground and shot off Very guns, piercing the night sky with fiery flares.

"The war is over!" chorused hundreds of voices.

"Oh, blessed relief," cried Jack. "Is it possible not to have that 'going-back' guillotine over my head?"

That Christmas the three Lewis men were together again at Little Lea. Each one seemed shocked at the sight of the other two. Warnie was shiny-faced from gin and going plump; Albert was pasty-faced and still erect at fifty-six, though it seemed only an effort to support his protruding stomach; and twenty-year-old Jack was told in blunt, worried tones that he was baggy-eyed and pencil-thin. Lapsing into morose silences, Jack knew now Little Lea was behind him. Warnie too was remote. He would return to France and await orders.

By January 13, 1919, Jack was back in "Univ" College in the golden-spired haven of Oxford University, but this time he was not alone. Mrs. Moore rented a house for Maureen and herself at 28 Warneford Road. The owner, Miss Featherstone, remained living in one small room. The old lady walked to morning prayers no matter how foul the weather and insisted on serving Mrs. Moore tea when she returned. A Christian actually trying to live the Gospel always deeply impressed Jack, but he assured himself it was only because he despised hypocrisy.

Jack quickly got in the routine of studying all morning, bicycling the two miles from Oxford to take lunch with Mrs. Moore, and then staying until late in the evening. At Mrs. Moore's insistence, most of his time there was spent studying. "We mustn't interrupt your studies. I'll let you know when it's eleven o'clock," she promised.

Then he returned to his rooms at "Univ." As he lay in bed, he heard chimes striking midnight and felt blessed. He would live and die for Oxford: the ubiquitous yellow-gray stone, the cozy book shops, the great vaulted halls, the unparalleled libraries, the poplars, the sleepy rivers. It seemed as safe and pure as Switzerland.

Post-war college life, however, was different. When he had departed for Officer Training, less than ten undergraduates had been in his college. Now "Univ" consisted of twenty-eight students, and was steadily building up to full strength. Only a few older alumni had survived the war to pass on "Univ" traditions to the newcomers. As a result of a coal shortage, only one lecture room, the library, and the Junior Common Room were cozy warm. Sometime in the future the undergraduates would once again be served breakfast and lunch in their rooms, but for now they were served all meals in the Hall. When the undergraduates assembled in the Junior Common Room to hold their first meeting, the war made itself shockingly evident.

"Look here!" exclaimed the secretary. "The minutes of the last meeting are from 1914!"

Jack was relieved to learn of one unexpected benefit of the war: the requirement to pass Responsions was waived for all veterans. Although Jack had failed this test earlier because of the math, now he would never have to retake it. Other hurdles loomed, however, his next one being "Honor Mods." He would be examined on Greek and Latin literature in his particular specialty: Classics. If he passed, his degree would be graded "First," "Second," or "Third." With the rigorous preparation of Kirk behind him, Jack thought he could pass it right away.

"Any future as a scholar requires a 'First,' " advised his tutor, Arthur Poynton, "and I don't believe you could get a 'First' just yet."

Poynton was a Fellow of about fifty, distinguished in the Classics, so Jack gladly took his advice. What was the hurry? Deferment and knowing he was enhancing knowledge already more than adequate certainly made studying less stressful. Beyond "Honor Mods" he would be studying ancient history and philosophy in the Classics for the second academic hurdle, "Greats." There too he determined to achieve a "First."

"Because my goal," he confided to Mrs. Moore, "is nothing less than getting a Fellowship and becoming an Oxford don."

As was the Oxford tradition, Jack met with his tutor Poynton only once a week for an hour. There he discussed what he had read. Actual attendance at the college was not heavy either. During the entire year the student had to be in residence only during three eight-week terms: the fall term, Michaelmas; the winter term, Lent; and the spring term, Easter. Jack was gratified to realize, however, that the serious students usually studied there during the so-called "vacations" too. Good. He would now have no reason to return to Little Lea and be with his father. He was disgusted with his father. Correspondence with him, which Jack did not mind, would be sufficient; he would add to his "diary" and also fulfill the sense of duty he sensed because he received support from his father.

"I receive all the affection I need from Mrs. Moore," he

assured himself.

In March of 1919, *Spirits in Bondage* was published by Heinemann. Reviews by newspapers were complimentary. The most important review in Jack's mind was the Literary Supplement of the *London Times*, known in his intellectual circles as the "TLS." It deemed his poetry "graceful and polished." His father's and Warnie's opinions of the book were remarkable in their breadth. Warnie liked the book, but he feared Jack was foolish to blatantly embrace atheism. To get ahead in England, a man had to believe in God and the king. On the other hand, father Albert had faint praise for the book but did not believe Jack was an atheist at all. Jack was some kind of dualist. An atheist would not write:

> *Yet what were endless lives to me*
> *If still my narrow self I be*
> *And hope and fail and struggle still,*
> *And break my will against God's will.[1]*

Sales of the book were anemic, but how many books of poetry sell well? At least the book gave Jack some recognition at Oxford. Some jokingly called him the "famous Lewis." To many others, he was the "mysterious Lewis." Who else bicycled off every day, disappearing for hours? Jack had to admit his passion for compartmentalizing his interests. Arthur depicted one world. Mrs. Moore embodied one world. Warnie represented one world. Little Lea symbolized one world. And Oxford epitomized yet another world. Only Arthur and Mrs. Moore were familiar with Jack's other worlds.

"Only rarely do my worlds meet," reflected Jack.

One of those rare occasions transpired in June of 1919 when Arthur visited Oxford. Since Arthur already knew much about Mrs. Moore, Jack took him straight to her, and she treated him like a son too. Soon she was talking with Arthur about starting a chicken farm!

"Capital idea," approved Arthur, who was the most receptive person Jack knew.

"I'm sure such a business venture requires the most careful planning," cautioned Jack, alarmed.

Jack remembered old letters to Arthur which had hinted that more than a mother/son relationship had developed between Mrs. Moore and himself. Observing Arthur, he realized he wouldn't have to explain that fabrication; Arthur was figuring it out. Now that Jack thought about the intimation, he realized the lie probably had made Arthur react the wrong way with his father, thus considerably contributing to the worsening relationship with his father. Jack recalled that he had also lied to Arthur about a Belgian girl who lived near Kirk by writing that he was intimate with her. Another adolescent lie. *Well,* Jack justified himself, *who doesn't lie about romance when they are young? I was only trying to make my letters steamy and interesting.*

By the end of Arthur's visit, Mrs. Moore had practically adopted him too. "She's a sweet thing to be sure," Arthur expressed to Jack.

"As sweet as a Minto," agreed Jack, referring to a popular candy. Thus, after Arthur's return to Ireland, he and Jack referred to Mrs. Moore as "Minto" in their letters. In spite of Jack's involved domestic life, he certainly did not neglect Oxford. He accepted an invitation to join a literary club called the Martlets. They invited only a dozen or so undergraduates. The Martlets introduced Jack to the kind of lofty world Oxford could be. They were talking about visiting John Masefield or William Butler Yeats! Masefield's strong narrative poetry was very popular. Talk of his becoming

England's Poet Laureate buzzed. Jack, on the other hand, much preferred Yeats. He adored Yeats' lyrical poetry based on pagan Celtic mythology.

"That I might be talking to Yeats. . ." fantasized Jack, almost unbelieving.

Over the months he met other undergraduates with similar interests, particularly poetry. Rodney Pasley, one of the most gregarious, was very impressed by Jack and virtually promoted him.

"Lewis is no ordinary undergraduate like the rest of us," praised Pasley. "He is quite an intimidating 'brain.'" Pasley further reasoned that his "discovery" of Lewis naturally warranted his introducing Lewis around. Soon Pasley had dozens talking about Jack.

Shortly, Jack met Leo Baker, Owen Barfield, and Cecil Harwood. All three men had started at Wadham College the fall term of 1919. Their razor-sharp dialectics, as well as their decency and honesty, reminded Jack of Laurence Johnson. Kirk would have approved of them. Jack felt he was bettering himself just being in the company of such gentlemen. Not that they were in any way sissified. The feisty chisel-jawed, wild-haired Barfield and Jack were at loggerheads immediately, and they were well matched.

"How can you have read all the right books," Jack pumped Barfield, "and formed all the wrong conclusions?"

"Lewis, you took the words right out of my mouth," Barfield parried.

Nonetheless, Barfield became Jack's second great friend; Arthur was the first. Arthur, however, was Jack's *alter ego*, agreeing with Jack in almost everything. He deviated from Jack at first only in liking very much everything—even the homely. Eventually, Jack had come to Arthur's viewpoint, reading novels that he never would have read otherwise, and enjoying the countryside he once would have dismissed with a glance. Barfield, by contrast, was Jack's negative image. If Jack said white, Barfield said black. If Jack said black, Barfield said white. Like Arthur, Barfield shared all of Jack's chief interests, but his conclusions were invariably and unmitigatedly opposite of Jack's. Amazingly, instead of repulsing each other, they eagerly anticipated their next argument!

"Out of these perpetual dogfights has emerged a strong friendship," he related to Mrs. Moore. "How I respect a man who can logically articulate his side and not back down."

To Jack, acceptable companions had to defend their opinions not only with logic, but also with feeling. Yet brilliant, passionate dialectics was not enough; any who displayed flippancy or cynicism were disqualified. Those who advanced only anecdotes or mere disjointed facts were held in lowest regard. Few people met his stringent standards.

Oxford provided a delightful place for debates between Jack and the handful who met his standards. In the winter they gathered around fireplaces. In all weather they took long walks on tree-lined paths and longer walks into the surrounding hills and vales. Walks were a way of life with Oxford gentlemen, either in solitude or in camaraderie. And for a man like Jack, who despised sports, his walks kept him fit. In warm weather, the coterie canoed or swam in the Cherwell River. In the most secluded area along the river, "Parson's Pleasure," they sunbathed and swam.

"Before breakfast every morning," Jack disclosed to Owen Barfield, "I go to Parson's Pleasure. I swim on my stomach toward the rising sun. Then I reverse direction, swimming on my back, gazing overhead at the willow trees. This is my ritual for 'washing the night off.' " Barfield had become as great a confidant as Arthur.

Jack was no longer willing to return to Little Lea unless Warnie was present to provide some cushion against Albert's prying. Understandably, because of Jack's insinuations, Albert remained suspicious of Jack's alliance with Mrs. Moore and obsessed by what it might mean. By letter he grilled Jack, then ambled across the street to interrogate Arthur. For this reason, Jack began instructing Arthur as to which part of Jack's letters were to be revealed to Albert during the inevitable interrogation. Later, by letter, Albert would pester Warnie, all the way off in France or Belgium or wherever he was posted at the time.

Jack resented his father more and more. Gentlemen simply did not pry into the private affairs of other men. Any attempt by another undergraduate to pry, subtly or otherwise, could so effectively turn Jack from a congenial companion into a shockingly angry antagonist that the trespasser never repeated the offense.

Pasley's remark about Lewis being an intimidating "brain" carried only half the truth. The other half was the overwhelming force of Jack's liberated intellect. The reticent student had clearly evolved into a formidable one. He was definitely the product of Kirk. The most casual remark was taken as a summons to debate. "I challenge that" and "On the contrary" were familiar phrases to Jack's companions. Jack reveled in the clash of logic like a fencer-lunge, thrust, parry, riposte, fleche!

He would even cry, "Touché!"

Ironically, his forceful intellect had been emancipated by the company of Mrs. Moore, who made him feel older and more sociable, and the company of men like Barfield, who made him feel like he was a good man too—as good as any. Now he was completely at ease with other undergraduates, free to unleash the relentless dialectics he had

65

learned from Kirk.

"You can't start your argument with God," he would suddenly erupt at an unsuspecting companion. "I don't accept God!"

When talking with Christians, he battered them with a stock of questions he considered unanswerable:

"Why did your God create a nature so immensely cruel?"

"Why would your God allow innocent animals to suffer pain?"

"Why does your God allow babies to die?"

"Why did your God make a vast universe with life on only one planet?"

"Why is your God's universe running down as the scientists say?"

"If your God is good and all powerful, why are so many of his creatures unhappy? Is He not loving?"

"Why is mankind always at war?"

Opponents who could withstand Jack's onslaught for a while were mentally graded by him as A's, B's, and C's. (Owen Barfield was at the top of a handful of A's.) Jack had no sympathy, however, for the poor souls who could not defend their assertions. These, he secretly dismissed as dolts.

By April 1920, Jack had taken a "First" in his Honor Mods, confirming his high standing among undergraduates. Only a very few received Firsts. He moved on to prepare for "Greats," an effort which entailed mastering Greek and Latin histories as well as philosophy.

He also moved in another direction. A student was allowed to live off campus after two terms. Many nights now he would not return to his rooms at "Univ" at all, choosing rather to stay in his own small bedroom in the house of Mrs. Moore at 28 Warneford Road. This arrangement was not a secret from his

closest friends, for Barfield, Baker, and Harwood frequented
the home for tea or late evening discussions. Mrs. Moore tactfully avoided the company, as was the custom of women
when men smoked pipes and chatted around a fireplace. Jack
made no attempt to deceive his friends or to explain his relationship with her. Some winter evenings he would rise during
a conversation and merely say, "I must fill Mother's hot water
bottles." He was sure they had come to understand that Mrs.
Moore was the closest thing he had to a mother and that he
was the closest thing she had to a son.

Only his father did Jack deceive about his relationship
with Mrs. Moore. Jack's anger with Albert was now a snarl
of resentments. He was still hurt over his father's refusal to
visit him when he had been recovering from his wounds. He
was angry over his father's obsessive snooping. Instead of
respecting Jack's silence on a subject, he pried and pried.
That he had to depend on Albert for money was agonizing
to Jack. What would happen if Albert uncovered the truth
about his arrangement with Mrs. Moore? He would protest,
then try to squelch it by withholding the money. *If Father
had been reasonable and a gentleman who minded his own
business,* Jack rationalized, *I would not have had to lie to
him.* It was as simple as that. His father's flaunted Christian
self-righteousness made him even more insufferable.

Early in 1921 two major events occurred in Jack's life, as
if to prove William Blake's assertion that life is "joy and
woe woven fine. . ."

six

Real Life

J ack received a terse telegram from his father. "Good heavens, Old Kirk died."

Smewgy had died during the influenza epidemic of 1918. Now Jack's second great mentor had died. In his head, Jack knew that Kirk would be the first to warn him not to be sentimental, but in his heart, Jack knew his intellectual weapons had been honed razor-sharp by the taskmaster Kirk. Who had made it possible for Jack to enter Oxford? Kirk. Who had taught Jack how to be unrelenting in his clarity of thought? Kirk. Who had taught him to be rigidly honest in his thought? Kirk. And what fine memories he cherished of the old man: his dry humor, his imperturbable good temper, his fiery energy! Few men measured up to Kirk.

"How he loved virtue," Jack fondly remembered, "and he was a man who did not accept God."

Paradoxically, many of Jack's friends embraced Christianity or, at the very least, theism, albeit Barfield and Harwood now embraced the anthroposophy of Rudolph Steiner, the Austrian scientist and philosopher. Steiner focused on the human being, not God. Man's spiritual capacity had been quelled by devotion to materialism, but the spiritual world was accessible to the properly developed intellect. To Jack, Steiner seemed no more than a Gnostic, an ancient sect of vain mystics. "Anthroposophy is somewhere between self-worship and irrational mumbo-jumbo," he needled Barfield.

Some of the sting of losing Kirk was dulled by a visit with the Irish poet, William Butler Yeats, at his residence at Number 4 Broad Street, just five minutes from Jack's rooms at "Univ." Jack and his colleagues ascended a long staircase along a wall lined with prints of devils and monsters engraved by the mystical genius William Blake before entering a room flickering with light from candles and a fireplace. A semi-circle of hardback chairs faced the blazing logs. In front of a bay window hung with orange drapes, a divan also faced the fire.

"Sit here, gentlemen," Mrs. Yeats waved Jack and the others into the hardback chairs.

Surprisingly, instead of Yeats, his wife seated herself on the divan while he selected one of the hardback chairs. Glasses magnified the already large face of the gray-haired poet in his late fifties. The giant—he was tall, broad, and corpulent—delivered a monologue, prodded on during any pauses by his wife's judicious questions. He spoke in a peculiar, stagy accent which sounded French to Jack. As Jack's ears became more familiar with the sounds, they began to sound Irish, even enchanted. Yeats' voice was perfect for his poetry. Jack was awed into complete silence. He felt as if he were part of some privileged circle listening to Samuel Johnson, even though Yeats was the antithesis of Johnson. Whereas Johnson was immensely sane, Yeats was so mystical he seemed insane. He spoke of magic and how some minds were not strong enough to handle it.

"I believe him," Jack finally sputtered under his breath.

Although Jack suppressed the temptation to make a point once in the monologue, later someone else made the same point. Yeats quickly and convincingly annihilated the argument. What a presence! Even Jack was overwhelmed. Yeats could have been a sorcerer. After a while Jack would have believed anything he said. To finish the evening, they drank sherry or vermouth in tall, grotesque glasses.

Later Jack reflected further on the shocking conversation he had heard from Yeats. Apparently, all the fantasy and myth Jack loved to read about were accepted as real by Yeats!

A week later Jack returned for another evening with Yeats. This time Yeats was not in a mystical mood at all. He engaged in a conversation as learned and low-key as a professor's. Regardless, Jack enjoyed him immensely.

Rather than feeling intimidated by the great poet as before, this time Jack was emboldened. "Do you like the prose fantasies of William Morris, sir?"

"Ah, I knew Morris well. Died about the time I left London in 1896. Yes, I like his fantasies."

His answer made Jack feel wonderful.

Later that spring of 1921, Jack's composition on "Optimism" won the Vice-Chancellor's prize for best English essay. In June Oxford held its graduation ceremony called Encaenia, which was attended by all the grandees. Participants wore not only full evening dress but caps and gowns of scarlet and blue and silver. The highlight of Encaenia this year was bestowing an honorary degree on the great French leader Clemenceau. As part of the ceremony, student prize-winners were to read two minutes of their winning essays. Jack's ego withered as he observed other prize-winners speak.

"Never have I seen such a collection of scrubby, beetle-like, bespectacled oddities," he tittered disparagingly.

Arthur Poynton, Jack's tutor, was delighted at Jack's success, since it was partly his too. Jack was surprised though by the reaction of his fellow undergraduates. Men he considered louts—defined by him as ignorant brutes who had too much money, excelled at sports, and unwittingly blocked passageways with their beefy bodies—congratulated him. There it was again. That civility that some possessed. Jack would never have congratulated them on a sports accomplishment. Abruptly Jack considered, *Perhaps I am the lout!*

One day in his Oxford rooms Jack was shocked by his mail. "Father is coming to Oxford in June!" he blurted. *After all these years!* he wondered silently. Maybe Old Kirk's death had jolted Albert. Albert, Uncle Augustus Hamilton, and his wife, Aunt Annie, would rent a car in Wales and tour England.

Since Jack kept his room at Mrs. Moore's, he had to make a choice now either to reveal the truth or concoct an elaborate lie. A small lie wouldn't suffice. With a sinking heart, Jack admitted that his father wouldn't be the only one disappointed in him. Aunt Annie was his favorite aunt, the aunt who had always been the comforter at Little Lea after his mother had died. She was the one who had packed his clothes for school and given him that soft, sweet-smelling hug good-bye. She had been the closest thing he'd had for a mother until Mrs. Moore had come along. How disappointed Aunt Annie would be! No explanation about Mrs. Moore would satisfy her. A substitute for her dear sister-in-law Flora? Indeed!

So Jack chose to lie. He wrote his father, saying he had been moved out of the college and was sharing an apartment with Rodney Pasley. He suggested his father and uncle and aunt make the quickest stop possible in Oxford because Rodney was studying day and night for exams. A much better and more relaxing option would be for him to leave Oxford with them and accompany them on part of the tour, he suggested. Albert agreed.

Jack's contempt for his father was never more glaring as he later wrote Warnie:

> *. . .the funniest piece of scenery I saw was. . .*
> *the Old Air Balloon himself. . .you have no*
> *idea how odd he looked, almost a bit shrunk;*
> *pacing alone with that expression peculiar to*
> *him on a holiday—the eyebrows halfway up*
> *the forehead. . .He seemed dazed by his sur-*
> *roundings and showed no disposition to go*
> *and see my rooms, though he observed that*
> *"the College had treated me very shabbily as*
> *they distinctly mentioned free rooms as one*
> *of the privileges of scholars". . .[1]*

Jack's letter to his father after Albert returned to Little Lea, however, revealed no trace of dissatisfaction:

> *I still feel that the real value of such a holiday*
> *is still to come, in the images and ideas which*
> *we have put down to mature in the cellarage*
> *of our brains, thence to come up with a con-*
> *tinually improving bouquet.[2]*

What was it that made Jack so duplicitous? Once again it seemed to be his compartmentalization. He and Warnie had always talked to each other that way about Albert. It was the remnants of childhood, the annoyance with a domineering, snoopy father. To judge from Jack's acid comments to Warnie, Albert was the most incompetent and comical of figures. In Jack's unguarded moments, though, he recognized that Albert was yet very forceful and articulate, the sire of the very forceful and articulate Jack himself. Furthermore, as the purse-holder, he still dominated part of Jack's life.

Even at 22, Jack felt no guilt for his deceit. "Nor shame," he bragged to Barfield. "Of your precious virtues of veracity, self-denial, and chastity, I think as a monkey thinks of Mozart."

After Albert's visit, which Jack believed would be his last for many years to come, Jack became domestic, cooking, cleaning, shoveling snow, and performing all the duties of an older son. Not only was he like a son to Mrs. Moore, but he was like an older brother to Maureen, helping her with school projects in woodworking and art. She was very bright and, at times, remarkably mature and tactful, but most of the time she was an exasperating adolescent. Yet, Jack could not be angry with her when he found her reading one of his favorite authors, George MacDonald!

Jack was becoming hospitable too. As much as he owed his intellect to Smewgy and Kirk, he owed his burgeoning gift of hospitality to Mrs. Moore. The threesome began entertaining more. Mrs. Moore's physician brother, John Askins, who lived nearby in Iffley, often visited. Gradually their circle of friends widened. Finally he had his Oxford friends coming to dinner. On these occasions, the ebullient Mrs. Moore shone, as perfect a hostess as her rice pudding. Although she voiced her opinions when she was alone with Jack, she remained silent or politely agreeable during his conversations with his friends. Jack was certain his friends now understood his affection for her and figured that the presence of teen-aged Maureen, astonishingly gracious and articulate, confirmed the innocence of his relationship with the Moores.

Some of the female guests were attracted to dark-haired, dark-eyed, ruddy-cheeked Jack. Though he had lost the gauntness of his war days, he supposed himself to be neither ugly nor handsome. All appearance aside, however, he was on the rise. And wasn't he available? One young lady attracted to him was Mary Wiblin, nicknamed "Smudge," a brilliant young woman who gave Maureen violin lessons in exchange for Jack's tutoring her in Latin. When he walked her home one night, she told him she loved him! He replied that he was too far from reaching his goals to consider marriage.

"She was crushed," he disclosed to Mrs. Moore later.

"Good grief, don't discourage young ladies so. Smudge would wait for you."

In June 1922 Jack took his "Greats" in Greek and Latin histories as well as Philosophy. The tests lasted six days. The candidate had to write two three-hour papers each day. The topics included Roman history, Greek and Latin translations, Philosophy, Plato, Aristotle, logic, general ancient history, Greek and Latin prose works, morals, and politics. Much emphasis was placed on skill in translating. Few could excel Jack at that. Years before, Kirk had told Albert that Jack was the most gifted translator he had ever known. Jack achieved "Firsts" again.

"Another scholastic triumph," bragged Mrs. Moore, concealing her inward edginess. Would Jack leave her? she wondered.

Many positions were now beckoning Jack. He had an offer from Cornell University in America, from Reading University in England, and even from Wadham College at Oxford, but the positions would require him to become a Law Tutor eventually. Jack's heart was set on a Fellowship at Oxford in the Classics or Philosophy because a Fellowship guaranteed a lifetime of fruitful work. Surely to one with his succession of Firsts, a Fellowship was inevitable. Once a Fellow, he would become one of the staff, a "don." But no Fellowship materialized!

Poynton commiserated with Jack. "A student these days, no matter how brilliant, rarely walks right from Greats into a Fellowship. Something will open up eventually. Be patient. In the meantime, take another Great. A First in English would make you very employable."

Jack was stunned. More studies? That meant he would have to ask his father for more money. And so he did:

> . . .*if, on all this, you feel that the scheme is rather a tall order and that my education has already taken long enough, you must frankly tell me so. . .(on the other hand) if you think that the chance thus offered can, and ought to be taken, I shall be grateful. . .*[3]

Jack awaited Albert's answer. Leo Baker, after passing Greats, also found no suitable position. The blow leveled the poor fellow, and he suffered a nervous breakdown. Now he too was living with Mrs. Moore. Taking him in had not been Jack's idea. Mrs. Moore, ever the hospitable mother, had insisted on it.

Meanwhile Jack and Owen Barfield, who also was one of the few to score Firsts, met for drinks at the "Old Oak" in Oxford. Barfield had composed a brilliant thesis titled, "Poetic Diction." When no Fellowship was offered, however, he floundered to the point of nearly giving up on the academic life. "I'll go into law," he yielded sourly.

Barfield returned to Jack the manuscript of a long narrative poem called *Dymer*. Jack didn't dare tell his friends he couldn't recall ever creating the story. It had simply appeared in his mind in its entirety when he had been an adolescent—not words, but images he had to describe. The experience had been magical. Regardless of the method, Barfield assured Jack that he liked it very much, Harwood had "danced with joy" over it, and Baker had raved about it. As usual they found something about which to argue. Jack asserted his theme of the poem—that too much dreaming destroys a man—was true.

Barfield immediately snapped, "I take the opposite view!" and the argument was on.

Sometime later Jack went on a walk in the countryside with Barfield and Harwood. Throughout their conversation they suggested several themes for *Dymer*: rejection of fantasy; danger of the occult; the cancer of totalitarian utopias and equally undesirable anarchy; and death and redemption. *Good heavens,* thought Jack, *does* Dymer *really have such a suffocating jumble of themes?*

Finally one of them joked, "Kipling was correct. Every single one of us is right!" Barfield promptly cavorted wildly in a field, startling some horses. Who could be miserable in such company? How Jack loved the company of decent men!

Albert finally answered Jack's request for more money by suggesting other options, primarily law and business. Jack flatly averred that an academic career was his only option. Hadn't Kirk said the same thing? Since Albert revered Kirk, he eventually agreed to continue supporting Jack. He would not permit Jack to stoop to second best, even in academics. If Jack wanted Oxford, so be it.

So Jack began his Great in English. He would now study for career the same works he had always read for pleasure: Chaucer, Shakespeare, Spenser, and dozens more. His first project was to learn Old English in order to master *Beowulf* and smaller gems like the haunting *Dream of the Rood*. Next, for the enchanting Medieval legends, he would study Middle English under C.T. Onions.

The Great in English was very demanding. His tutor was Frank Wilson, a plump man of about thirty, at Exeter College. He rather doubted that Jack could get through the Great for

English in nine months as he desired, but he did not know how readily Jack picked up languages. For Kirk, he had mastered Italian in seven weeks. In no time at all, he had become adept in Old English and now was zipping through English Literature, which was no less than the history of England. In general, Jack felt his old friends, Barfield and Harwood, could have thrashed the students at Exeter, but for one exception: a very forceful, brilliant classmate in a discussion class led by the scholar George Gordon, Nevill Coghill.

During one discussion, Coghill proposed, "Mozart remained a child of six his entire life."

"I can't imagine anything more delightful," chuckled Jack.

Coghill's interest was sparked. Later, over beer at an inn, the tall, lean Coghill cautiously scrutinized Jack, "Are you an Irish Republican?"

"No," Jack responded, "I'm an Ulster Irishman, just like you."

Discussion of their war experiences followed. "I fought in the trenches at Arras," recalled Jack, "but I loathed the war."

"I was a gunner at Salonika," revealed Coghill, "but I got my worst fright in Ireland. The Republicans dragged me out of my house one night and stood me in front of a firing squad. Then, abruptly, they released me. The whole thing was intended only to terrorize me."

"Ah, so that's why you asked if I was a Republican," Jack nodded. "What a violent world we live in."

While Coghill was not the dialectician Jack and his other friends were, he had a very powerful, artistic mind and was inclined toward the theater. *Wonder of wonders,* mused Jack, *Coghill is a Christian too! Why are all the most brilliant students believers? Except me. . .*

Meanwhile Barfield hung around Oxford, picking up jobs editing for small magazines, in an effort to stave off the practice of law. Other friends of Jack, however, were deserting Oxford. For instance, Harwood, deep into Steiner's anthroposophy, was setting up a school. Rodney Pasley had become headmaster at a public school. Leo Baker, recovered from his breakdown, had taken a fling at acting in the local theater groups in Oxford, then traded Oxford's limited opportunities for the actor's Mecca: London.

In August Warnie visited Jack. "I patiently await release from my 'imprisonment' in the army," he repined. "I acknowledge Wordsworth my master, wanting only 'tranquillity to all things' and 'peaceful days for their own sakes, as mortal life's chief good.'"

Although Warnie now seemed peculiarly eccentric and reclusive to Jack, Warnie was not the one who had changed. Jack had changed, thanks to Mrs. Moore. As if to remind Jack how unsociable he had once been, Warnie refused to stay with them, and instead chose a hotel. He also declined an invitation to tea. Then Warnie abruptly changed his mind and agreed to stay at the house.

In the days that followed, he socialized pleasantly with the Moores and several young ladies who were frequently there, including Smudge, and joined their excursions enthusiastically. Jack expected Warnie to collapse during the two weeks of rowing, walking, bicycling, and tennis-playing, but he held his own. Though much heavier than before, he was more fit than he looked. Jack was very pleased with the way things worked out. To Warnie's great surprise—but not to Jack's—Mrs. Moore insisted that after Warnie left the Army he had to live with them!

"I say, Jack," Warnie commented as he was leaving, "you needn't have arranged such a violent social life on my account."

"Don't pride yourself, Arch-Piggy-Bottom," Jack teased. "Our house is always like this."

Domestic life continued to flourish, especially after Jack and the Moores moved into a respectable brick home in Headington, a village east of Oxford. This house earned the name "Hillsboro." As if Jack didn't have enough turmoil in Oxford, Aunt Lily, his mother's older sister, came to live in a cottage in Forest Hill. Now widowed, she was somewhat overwhelming like Mrs. Moore, but in a bizarre way. In just three days, she had instigated several run-ins and had written a fiery letter to the local newspaper. Her greatest passion was for animals.

"Pekingese are not dogs at all, but lions bred tiny through the centuries," she informed Jack.

"I didn't know that," Jack acquiesced politely.

Aunt Lily was a bubbling volcano of facts, speculation, and pure blather. She liked Jack very much because, as she said, she rarely found her intellectual equal. She and Albert were not on speaking terms. As she referred to him as "ignorant Allie," Jack quietly relished her hostility toward his exasperating father.

"Mistreating animals is wrong," she sputtered about her favorite subject. "I once broke a man's arm with his own horsewhip for beating the poor beast."

"Yes, and there are those poor pit ponies in the coal mines," bemoaned Jack sympathetically. "Not to mention the poor children who must work there."

"Oh, don't mention the children!" Aunt Lily charged. "They just grow up to be brutes themselves."

By 1923 Jack was trying to become a completely rational man. He allowed himself to be drawn to psychology and determined to put aside the romantic myths that had attracted him so much when he was younger. As he pondered the fact that he and his talented friends, despite having amassed Firsts, were not finding positions, he suffered spells of dread. He also began doubting his own poetry. Owen Barfield had apprised him bluntly that he wrote too much and revised too little. Barfield saw clearly that Jack, capable of writing the very finest sort, wrote much that was not fine at all. "Slow down," counseled Barfield. "Revise." In his heart Jack knew Barfield, the finest mind he knew, was right; he was right about nearly everything. Yet heedlessly, Jack raced ahead with his poetry.

"*Dymer* will put an end once and for all to my shabby desire for some 'otherness,'" he reassured himself.

Dymer, his long narrative poem, would make clear that fantasizing made men weak. Men retreated within themselves. His hero in the poem was a dreamer who realized in the end that his dreams had caused chaos, and that his redemption lay only in fighting a monster that would surely kill him. Jack wrote four cantos of the poem. Free verse was the fashion, but his gadfly, Barfield, had convinced him that sometimes ancient things are superior to modern things and to think otherwise was mindless modern prejudice. So Jack wrote poetry the way he wished to read it himself. He rhymed and scanned and constructed complex stanzas.

A real-life example of the danger of fantasizing, or probing the edges of the spirit world, hit Jack right at home. The victim was none other than John Askins, Mrs. Moore's physician brother. "Doc" had dabbled in theosophy, spiritualism, yoga, and every aspect of the occult. He had once seemed to Jack a living testimony that such endeavors were safe. In early 1923, however, Doc began acting peculiar and talking about death.

"If one really thought about what awaits us, he couldn't last one hour in this world," Doc agonized ominously. Jack was nonplussed. To him, Doc was "the most unoffending, gentle, and unselfish man imaginable."

Each day Doc worsened. Then suddenly he was so bad, screaming and moaning about hell, that he was moved into their Hillsboro house. Doc's wife Mary needed help with his "fits." Doc had to be watched constantly and physically restrained during his wild seizures. Since Mrs. Moore's other brother Rob, in Bristol, was also a physician, he arrived and arranged for Doc, who was a veteran, to be taken into a Pensions Hospital. They were informed they would have to wait ten days for approval!

"Please, don't send me to hell ahead of time!" Doc would scream as they tried to subdue him. "Don't shorten my time here on earth!"

The next days were unremitting torment as Doc seemed to improve, then slip again, each time becoming more hopeless. He became so much more threatening, and his resistance was so much more violent that sleep for the others was nerve-racking. Would Doc leap upon one of them in the middle of the night with a knife or an ax? Jack wondered.

seven

Fellow in English

The inhabitants of Hillsboro house felt like they had not slept for weeks by the time the taxi finally came to transport Doc to the hospital. He screamed, he fought, he spit, he collapsed and became rigid. But at last he was gone. He had stayed at the house fourteen days. Three weeks later he died. That such a peaceful, mild-mannered man could be so transformed into a kicking, screaming maniac and slide into hell, either self-made or real, frightened Jack into holding tight his shaky rationalism.

"Surely my own glimpses of joy are a trap. But doesn't that mean I am admitting the existence of some spiritual power? And what of my nightmares? Where do they come from? If only I didn't remember them."

His latest was so vivid he felt compelled to record it in his diary. He, with friends, ascended a hill and came upon a wolf eating a sheep. After the wolf ran off, they cut up the sheep and began eating it. All the while the sheep screamed like a human being. . .

From childhood Jack had suffered from nightmares. Gnashing, clawing beetles had been succeeded by merciless maniacs at public school. Then for years he had relived real horrors of war. Now in his dreams he seemed to be fighting Satan and his minions. But how could a rationalist believe in the devil? Just where did these nightmares come from? Jack wailed within himself. Was there no relief from the bogies of life even in bed? Where was peace? He became quite depressed. Often he daydreamed now and his thoughts were morbid.

"Sometimes I daydream of being an old, successful man of genius, just awaiting death," he confessed to Mrs. Moore.

"That's silly. You're a mere twenty-four. Will you sand-paper the front stairs for me today?" she asked, dismissing his musings.

How could anyone study successfully while such turmoil writhed inside? Yet, later in 1923, Jack triumphed with a First in his Great in English. Of all the candidates in all thirty-five colleges at Oxford only he of "Univ" and Nevill Coghill of Exeter College got Firsts. Jack was confident now that he would obtain some position at Oxford. But days of expectation became weeks. Then weeks became months. Jack graded papers and tutored to earn a bit of money. Money had never been so short for him and the Moores. He tried to borrow money from Warnie, but learned that in nearly ten years of military service Warnie had saved not a penny. In fact, Warnie had wrangled a stipend from Albert!

Jack gave up smoking. The Hillsboro household gave up their maid, her household duties assumed by Jack more than anyone else. Gregarious Mrs. Moore could not help having guests as she always did though. And what was a home without dogs and cats—five in all? Jack shrugged. He wasn't starving. Once while walking he had been called "Heavy Lewis," and the nickname had stuck among his detractors. It was certainly true. He was now as plump as Warnie had appeared to him the year before.

His misery was deepened, of all things, by a visit from Arthur. Someone had convinced Arthur to be his natural self and satisfy his desires.

"But isn't that contrary to your Christian beliefs?" queried Jack at the dinner table.

"Not at all. Besides, Christianity is just being kind to one another—more or less." Arthur leaned back in his chair and put his feet on the table. "I say, don't you have some butter here? I loathe margarine."

Further discussions revealed Arthur now believed in heaven, but not hell. Jack was appalled at Arthur's blasé and simple-minded beliefs. How had he overlooked them before? Arthur's faults had never been more objectionable, his manners more incorrigible. After Arthur returned to Ireland, Jack could scarcely bring himself to write him any more, partly because of Arthur's disgusting new personality, and partly because he fed Jack's love for "otherness." Jack was determined, since Doc's death, to purge his love for "otherness."

Jack dropped Leo Baker because of Doc too. "How do you suppose Leo Baker is faring in London?" Mrs. Moore wondered to Jack one day.

"We're not likely to find out," Jack growled. "I wrote the ingrate and told him I did not want to see him or hear from him again. Ever!" Baker had not acknowledged Doc's death in any way. To Jack that was an unforgivable insult to Mrs. Moore who had cured Baker's nervous breakdown in her very own home.

One year after Jack finished his Great in English, he was waiting eagerly for a Fellowship in Philosophy at Trinity College. Meanwhile "Univ" offered Jack a year's position as tutor in Philosophy. He would replace a Fellow on sabbatical to America. What choice did Jack have? He was hanging on to Oxford by a mere thread. He wrote his father that he would give fourteen lectures next term, a total of fourteen hours, and joked that he could exhaust his total knowledge of philosophy in only five hours. His assigned subject was "The Moral Good." He had never worked harder to prepare. He pored over Hobbes, Hume, and one of his favorites, Henri Bergson. Somehow Bergson reinforced his new outlook. One must not nit-pick futilely over the very idea of existing but deal realistically with the material world.

To someone who tried to explain God to him, Jack snapped cynically, "It seems to me God is a being who spends His time in having His existence proved and disproved."

He was now a don—at least temporarily, and was required to live at "Univ" during the week. Thus, he stayed at Mrs. Moore's only on the weekends now. Breakfast at Oxford was served in his rooms. Besides his lectures, he gave tutorials in the morning, took lunch at Mrs. Moore's, did odd jobs around Hillsboro house, then returned to Oxford for more tutorials and dinner. Once again he dined in the great Hall, but now he dined among the dons sitting at the dais on one end. He wore a gown, something that was second nature to him after six years.

Heinemann rejected his manuscript of *Dymer*. Jack felt like his career in poetry was dying. Perhaps his Oxford career was dying too. All year he applied for every opening at Oxford in both Philosophy and English. One opening was at Magdalen College. He debated about applying for such a choice position because many men his senior were applying, even his old English tutor, Wilson. Eventually Jack half-heartedly applied anyway. Soon he found out Wilson had not applied. That had been a rumor. Jack rushed to Wilson to ask him for a recommendation. Wilson apologized. Because he had heard Jack had given up English for Philosophy, Wilson had glowingly recommended Nevill Coghill of Exeter, Jack's main rival in English. Jack was certain he had no chance now. Coghill was truly Jack's equal, and now he even had a recommendation from Jack's own tutor!

"How long can I hang on?" he lamented.

Then he received great news. Coghill had received a Fellowship from his old college, Exeter, and had withdrawn his application for Magdalen. Wilson enthusiastically recommended Jack. Was there still a chance? Would good fortune strike at last?

When Jack was invited to a dinner in May with the other candidates, however, he botched the invitation. Jack appeared in white tie and long tails; all the others wore black ties and dinner jackets. Somehow he survived the blunder, then surprisingly learned that he was one of two candidates remaining. In a week of very gloomy weather, he became doubtful again when he saw the other candidate, who couldn't conceal his absolute conviction that he had won. Jack's hope fell further when he was summoned by the President of Magdalen College in a curt note, then kept waiting outside his office half an hour. The future did not look promising.

But when he exited the President's office he muttered through a relieved smile, "Thank goodness, he's just a brusque man by nature." Jack had received a five-year appointment as Fellow in English at Magdalen College.

Immediately he wrote his father. A future of financial independence seemed to free Jack of his bitterness toward Albert. For years he had corresponded with duplicity. Now he truly felt grateful:

> . . .let me thank you from the bottom of my heart for the generous support, extended over six years, which alone has enabled me to hang on till this. In the long course I have seen men at least my equals in ability and qualifications, fall out for lack of it. . .You have waited, not

*only without complaint but full of encourage-
ment, while chance after chance slipped away
and when the goal receded farthest from sight.
Thank you again and again. . .*[1]

Free at last, he felt guilt at last. Even though his father had
held the purse strings, Jack had justified his resentment
because his father snooped and pried. Now Jack realized
his resentment had been much more. He resented Albert's
bluster. He resented Albert's insight. He resented Albert's
neurotic home-boundness. He resented the way Albert
raised his eyebrows. Every one of Albert's mannerisms
exasperated him. But why? He heartily enjoyed Aunt Lily's
eccentricities, and they were far more outrageous than any
Albert displayed!

"Father always supported me," Jack told Mrs. Moore. "I
feel such guilt."

"You'll get over it. Just think: at last you are an Oxford
don!" Mrs. Moore paused. "Could you lay the new linoleum
in the kitchen today?"

When Jack returned to Little Lea in September, his visit
with Albert was relaxed, even without Warnie and Arthur as
buffers. Warnie wasn't there, and the "new-and-improved"
Arthur was of little interest to Jack now. (Even the "old"
Arthur, because he fed Jack's fantasy too much, would have
been off limits.) When Jack returned to England, he felt pleasure at being able to decline Albert's offer to pay his passage.

At Oxford Jack lived in his rooms at Magdalen College
full time during the term. His only regular visits to Mrs.
Moore were for lunch. His rooms—on the second floor of
the three-story New Building—were splendid, even though
"new" meant new in 1733! Because Magdalen was built
outside the city walls to the east, it was the most spacious

and the most unfettered of all Oxford colleges. Jack's three white-paneled rooms on the east end of the second floor seemed the most unfettered of all. He wrote his father:

> *My external surroundings are beautiful*
> *beyond expectation and beyond hope. . .My*
> *big sitting room looks north, and from it I see*
> *nothing, not even a gable or spire, to remind*
> *me that I am in town. I look down on a stretch*
> *of level grass which passes into a grove of*
> *immemorial forest trees, at present colored*
> *autumn red. Over this stray the deer. . .Some*
> *mornings when I look out there will be half a*
> *dozen chewing the cud just underneath me. . .*
> *or one little stag. . .standing still and sending*
> *through the fog that queer little bark. . .a*
> *sound. . .I hear. . .day and night. . .*[2]

His smaller sitting room and his bedroom looked south across the broad lawn to a great Cloister Quadrangle and the ancient Magdalen Tower. This was paradise, and he had even forgotten to mention the River Cherwell that bordered Magdalen on the east and stretched north before his eyes too. In spite of being required to furnish bed, carpets, tables, chairs, sofa, fire irons, coal box, and drapes—which consumed about one-fifth his annual salary—he was certain his years of struggle were over.

"A great irony is that, except for Coghill who I don't see that often, all my closest friends at Oxford are gone," he confided soberly to Mrs. Moore.

So daily he tutored and lectured English and ate and talked with new colleagues. Only a few, like C.T. Onions, who had taught Jack Middle English, were acquaintances from the past. (Fondly, Jack recalled that the teacher had stammered until he quoted verse. Then the stammer evaporated, and he was superb.) Onions, about fifty now, was also one of five outstanding colleagues Jack admired at Magdalen, the others being C.C.J. Webb, F.E. Brightman, P.V.M. Benecke and J.A. Smith. Any one of them would say, "Oh yes, you'll find what you want in such and such," to any question Jack asked.

Chief among the five were Benecke and Smith. Paul Benecke, fifty-seven, very tall and angular, taught Classics. Handsome to a fault, he was also righteous, and both were reasons for many men to dislike him. He was a teetotaler, he fasted, and he never missed a church service in Chapel. Although he spoke often on any subject out of conscience, he rambled in a nervous, unhappy voice and was, consequently, ineffective as a debater. Despite that, Jack found himself drawn to Benecke and his overt Christianity and sat with him often at meals.

Under his gown, Benecke dressed poorly. His only extravagance was his collection of miniature pigs: stuffed, ceramic, wood, glass, ivory. His holiness showed through best when he talked of animals. "The melancholy in a dog's eyes is from its pity for men," he informed Jack one day.

J.A. Smith, even taller, older and more sober looking than Benecke, taught Philosophy and was an authority on Aristotle. As a moralist, he often made pronouncements, but as a philosopher, he was very slippery, not arguing directly. He had also become, through the years, a philologist, one who cherishes the history and meaning of words. He was an entertaining raconteur like Jack's father Albert. And to top it all off, J.A. knew Norse mythology. Jack rarely missed a chance to talk to him, aware of the paradox:

traits irritating in his father were endearing in others.

Jack did not like some of the other dons at all. Although Thomas Weldon was also a veteran of the trenches, Jack only talked reluctantly to the younger don. He was a philosopher and very close to Jack in his beliefs, yet Jack found him thoroughly disagreeable. He was cynical, scorning all creeds. But one night he shocked Jack.

Referring to the *Golden Bough* he urged, "Forget Fraser's dying God!" He hesitated. Nothing he had said so far had surprised Jack at all. "I've been reading the New Testament," continued Weldon, sounding apologetic. "It almost looks like it really happened."

"What!" exclaimed Jack. "You can't believe that."

"Oh, but I've thought it all through. More than once. I've been in war. Men don't willingly sacrifice themselves for a hoax. His followers did that only because they had seen him risen. There's other evidence as well. Worst luck!"

Jack was stunned. Christianity was only a myth—and a sorry one at that. But what if it wasn't? He had read G.K. Chesterton's *Everlasting Man*, and found his argument fascinating. Either Christ was Who He said He was—the Son of God—or He was an absolute lunatic. And Christ didn't sound like a lunatic—not even to the most cynical man alive!

Uncomfortable, Jack shrugged off the temptation. He had purged himself of otherness and dreams and myths. He operated in the real world now. He was unpleasantly reminded of *Dymer*, his work that showed the folly of dreaming. How many days, weeks, months had he labored on it? Yet it was stalled, its lack of fruition haunting Jack like a dying friend. With Barfield too remote now for advice, Jack turned to Nevill Coghill at an English faculty meeting in February 1926. Almost apologetically, Jack asked him to look at *Dymer*.

To Jack's astonishment, Coghill raved about it, proclaiming Jack to be another Masefield. Jack could not keep quiet. "Aren't you bothered by the theme: 'Too much dreaming destroys a man'?"

"Not at all. Besides, it is only one of several themes." Coghill paused tactfully. "In another of your themes you redeem the man through his dying in a final battle against his own offspring."

"That has nothing to do with Christianity, if that's what you are thinking," Jack interrupted. "Redemption though death is a common theme in myths." But Jack was no longer so certain. Barfield had liked *Dymer* too; his only complaint had been Jack's lack of polish.

Then, most incredible of all, Coghill located a publisher for Jack! On April 1, J.M. Dent and Sons accepted *Dymer*. What a relief for Jack to have his creation off and running. Now he could focus on other business.

On May 11, Jack attended a meeting of English dons to discuss the English curriculum. The meeting, at first hopelessly disjointed to Jack, finally evolved into a struggle between those who wanted to emphasize languages and those who wanted to emphasize literature. One pale, slender don in his mid-thirties cornered Jack after the meeting. "Language is the thing," he insisted. "English is not the study of history but the study of languages. From day one."

"I suppose you would have everyone learning Icelandic?" growled Jack, who favored the emphasis on literature.

"Certainly," rejoined the don.

"Good heavens!" Jack glared, exasperated, at Exeter's don of Old English: J.R.R. Tolkien. That he was bright, Jack had to admit, but he needed to be taken down a peg or two. On learning more about Tolkien, however, Jack no longer wondered how the man was almost one hundred percent wrong.

Tolkien was another Christian, and apparently practiced his faith. Jack cautioned himself to carefully protect his hard-earned realistic view of life. On the side, he was currently reading about the philanthropist Hannah More. Though she had started out a solid humanist, she fell into the snare of Samuel Johnson, and probably John Wesley as well. Eventually the poor woman ended up firmly in the quick-sand of Christianity. Yes, he would have to be very careful.

In July he found himself reading Morris's *The Well at the World's End* again. "There it is!" he wagged his head. "I triggered the old 'joy,' that brief, very satisfying glimpse into something beyond."

Why had he done that? He guarded against that. It wasn't consonant with his newfound rationalism, or humanism, or whatever he wanted to call it. The truth was that his intellectual state was a thorough muddle. He had passed through a smorgasbord of ideas and glutted on all sorts of them, ideas that seemed now to disagree with him. He had tasted scraps of Barfield's anthroposophy, bits of the new psychoanalysis, great chunks of Kirk's rationalism, Yeat's fairy world, and Arthur's Northernness. "Now even my rationalism is shaky," he shook his addled head. "Good riddance to Barfield and his ilk!"

Owen Barfield had planted the seed, the terrible notion that—aside from supernatural influence—there is no satisfactory explanation of knowledge for man. Knowledge depends on the validity of reason. "The new naturalists with their explanation of the natural universe as a totally accidental, random thing have shot themselves in the brain," Barfield had insisted. This random process could not validate reason. Why would anyone believe random electrical processes in the brain could yield reason and knowledge? Yet, nearly all men admit reason and knowledge are real.

"So what is the source of that reason?" Jack grilled himself. "Once again I've come back to spirit." He gritted his teeth. "Barfield!"

Jack's great love, literature, chafed him too. Why did he revel so in George MacDonald? MacDonald wasn't even a first-rate writer. Like Fielding, he somehow mounted such a forceful story—in MacDonald's case, something akin to a myth—that it overcame the bad writing. And then there were the top-drawer writers like Chesterton and Samuel Johnson and Spenser and Milton and Bunyan. Their writings were deep and rich, imminently truthful about everyday life. They were towers of reason and sanity. Yet they were Christians! And why was he so deeply moved by *Dream of the Rood*? And Dante, Langland, John Donne, and George Herbert? These men too were Christians.

And what of the greatest humanists, most of whom were atheists? George Bernard Shaw, H.G. Wells, John Stuart Mill, Gibbon, and Voltaire? Why did their works seem so thin and cheap, so devoid of real meaning for everyday life?

"Oh, my problem is much worse than that!" agonized Jack. He had looked recently at his own *Dymer*, which still seemed to him a withering rejection of fantasy, and despised it!

And what of his friends? Weren't his very best, brightest friends all Christians, or at least theists? Barfield. Harwood. Coghill. Good old Laurence Johnson. Even good—but—spoiled childish Arthur.

And which Magdalen faculty members did he eagerly seek out at meals? Paul Benecke and J.A. Smith—the Christians, of course.

Dymer was published in September, 1926. Jack again employed his pseudonym, Clive Hamilton. Reviews were good; sales were not. *Such is the lot of some poets,* reasoned Jack. Wasn't understanding the scope of literature his charge? Some poets were discovered and championed hundreds of years later, William Blake and John Donne, for instance. Jack ached inside, not sure he wanted to claim *Dymer* in the first place. It seemed more to belong to a confused cynic like Weldon than himself.

Another narrative poem Jack was creating only added to his confusion. Should he continue working on it or not? His time was so limited. He had started it in Bristol in 1918. By 1920 it had evolved into a poem he called "Wild Hunt." By 1924 it had haunted him enough that he had revised it yet again. It was now called "King of Drum."

"Why don't you come to the Kolbitars, Jack?" asked C.T. Onions one day late in 1926.

"The name sounds suspiciously Norse," Jack hazarded.

"It's Icelandic for 'coal-biters.' It means those who sit so close to the fire they can almost bite the coals. Tolkien organized it. . ."

"Tolkien." Jack humphed, then shook his head.

"We're reading the Icelandic sagas in the original," Onions recounted. "George Gordon is there. Nevill Coghill. Myself."

"Coghill? You?" Jack verified.

As Onions explained how they tackled the sagas, the process of learning seemed absolutely Kirkian. Jack had certainly thrived in that procedure. But Icelandic?

Onions, observing Jack's hesitation, chuckled. "The Norse legends are much more exciting than the original Greek legends."

"How so?" challenged Jack.

"Their gods are heroes. Their gods die."

"Then why does no one other than a few stuffy professors know the Norse legends?" posed Jack just to be difficult. He knew the answer. Besides, the pale little Tolkien was behind it.

"The Norse never had a Homer. Their stories are poor poetry."

"I'll think about it," Jack conceded.

He already knew German and Old English, and would probably pick up Icelandic fast. Oh, to read the Norse mythologies in the original. What Northernness! It was tempting. But would it endanger his rationalism? No, surely not. This would not be an indulgence for "joy"; this would be academic. Nonetheless, he was sick inside as he remembered the confused, miserable state of his rationalism.

That Christmas found both Jack and Warnie at Little Lea. For once, the days passed peacefully. Who had changed? Albert or his sons? Albert did not appear well. The old scathing comments about him behind his back lost their flavor to the brothers. Besides, Jack had the Kolbitars in the back of his mind all the while. *As if I don't have enough reading already!* But he could not resist the lure of those fiery coals. . .

eight

God's Grace

When Jack returned to Oxford, he recorded his feelings in a diary he had kept sporadically since 1922, about the time he had decided the "diary" he was leaving with his father at Little Lea was too restricted:

> *I got into a tremendously happy mood,*
> *what with the joy of being home again,*
> *and certain vague anticipations of good*
> *things beginning and a general sense of*
> *frosts breaking up. . .birds were making a*
> *great noise as if it was spring. . .*[1]

Mrs. Moore's health was not good. Now fifty-five, her eyes were going bad, and she had frequent headaches and bouts of rheumatism. Maureen was past adolescence, but often mother and daughter would fight, dragging Jack in as arbitrator. Then both were unhappy with him. As if that were not enough, they boarded Dotty Vaughan, who was attending Headington School with Maureen. A wild, coltish young woman, Dotty was ten times more boisterous and difficult than Maureen. Worse, Mrs. Moore spoiled her. When Dotty pestered for larger and larger picnics, then larger and larger parties, Mrs. Moore indulged her. . .because Dotty was just like Mrs. Moore: ebullient, extravagant, generous, hospitable.

"On top of all that," complained Jack, "I alone have to take the dog, Mister Papworth, out every day for his walk."

All complaints aside, he was delighted to be back at Oxford. He was keenly anticipating participation with the Kolbitars. On January 28, Jack borrowed J.A. Smith's *Icelandic Reader*. Soon Jack was hammering his way through the first chapters of *Younger Edda*. The first glimpses of the very words for "god" and "giant" in Icelandic ignited the old thrill and threw him back fifteen years into vast northern skies and Wagnerian music. The memory was deliciously poignant. Jack could hardly believe after all these years that he was going to read his early loves in their original language. "It's a good thing this is purely academic," he reassured himself.

That spring of 1927, Jack joined in a walking tour through the Wiltshire and Berkshire Downs with Owen Barfield, Cecil Harwood, and "Wof" Field. They wore twenty-pound packs and walked briskly. The goal every day was to end up at an inn for a delightful dinner. Nothing fancy. Quite the opposite. Just good boiled beef and bitter ale from wooden casks. To be first rank, the inn had to have wooden tables, tops waxed. In cold weather a wood fire was preferred. All the while they ambled, they breathed the outdoors. And of course they joked and argued. Jack was in his element: he was opposed by three anthroposophists!

"I am the bow-wow dogmatist," Jack described the quartet to Mrs. Moore later. "Owen Barfield is dark and labyrinthine. 'Wof' is as keen as a greyhound. And Cecil is just Cecil: serene in spite of it all."

Walking tours became annual spring events for Jack and his friends. In 1928 the same group walked through the Cotswolds, west of Oxford. Friendships were such joy.

The privileged life Jack had so ardently courted expanded his world, but it also came with unwelcome duties. Many of the students he tutored seemed impossibly backward. He had no Christian charity, so he felt no guilt calling them "fools" and "lumps" and worse in his diary. One overconfident student particularly got under Jack's skin: John Betjeman. On one occasion Betjeman showed up for his tutorial wearing gaudy bedroom slippers. "I hope you don't mind," he whined in lame politeness.

"I should mind very much if I were wearing them," snapped Jack with revulsion, "but I don't mind at all if you wear them." Eventually, Betjeman gave up and left Oxford with no degree.

At times, however, the faculty irritated Jack as much as the students. The scrap between languages and literature in the English curriculum persisted. Although he was changing his mind about J.R.R. Tolkien and actually beginning to like him, that only deepened his concern. Tolkien was very competent. As such, he might succeed in getting languages to be a major portion of the English curriculum.

Eclipsing all the aggravations was the announcement that the President of Magdalen would retire in November, 1928. Hogarth, every don's choice as successor, suddenly died. Intending to push his own agenda, Weldon, the cynical philosopher, put forward Chelmsford. Others put forward Paul Benecke, the Classicist Jack admired so much in spite of his being a Christian. The campaign became ugly.

Jack wrote Barfield:

> *This college is a cesspool, a stinking puddle, inhabited by things. . .in men's shapes climbing over one another and biting one another in the back, ignorant of all things except their own subjects and often even of those; caring nothing less for learning; cunning, desperately ambitious, false friends, nodders in corners,*

> *tippers of the wink; setters of traps and solic-*
> *itors of confidence; (a pox) upon them—*
> *excepting always the aged who have lived*
> *down to us from a purer epoch. . .²*

Jack could not bring himself to acknowledge that "purer epoch" as Christian, but he knew the young dons were the ones who had turned the campaign ugly. When forty-seven-year-old George Gordon was ultimately elected, Jack was pleased with the choice. The thought that all the good men were old and would pass on one way or another lingered and haunted him. Jack had no desire to be left solely among rationalists.

"But there I go again!" he exclaimed to Mrs. Moore. "Voicing my paradox! Shouldn't I want the Christians to pass on? Shouldn't I want the rationalists like myself to dominate?"

"Could you move the furniture in the setting room around for me tomorrow?" she answered.

Why does the ancient world seem civilized and the modern world barbaric? Jack's own internal war never abated. Above all, he was old Kirk's dialectician. The truth was he no longer believed in materialism and rationalism. They simply did not explain the human experience. Man's possession of logic required a cosmic logic, yet he still could not bring himself to call that logic "God." Jack's deeper study of philosophy shocked him further.

"O-o-oh!" he snarled through clenched jaws. "Of the philosophers and their Ultimates, only Berkeley's 'God' fits my new thinking. And I don't accept God."

While he did not read for that purpose, much of his reading illuminated his new suspicion of a supernatural influence. More and more of the great thinkers were reinforcing the supernatural. *Hippolytus* by Euripides annihilated his last remnants of rationalism. Suppressing emotion and spirit was folly. Jack craved again that other-worldliness that thrilled him with joy. Samuel Alexander's *Space, Time, and Deity* convinced him that his "joy" was not something he could contemplate. Rather, it was a mental track left by the passage of joy. Jack had been wrong about desiring just the brief glimpse itself. The "passage of joy" was a tiny moment of clearest consciousness when Jack ached for reunion with the utter reality, the Absolute.

"Whatever that is. Certainly not God," he objected uncomfortably.

Night after night, alone in his rooms at Magdalen, he resisted the identity, the reality of the Absolute. Then in the spring of 1929, he was riding a bus in Oxford. Suddenly without words or images, he felt at bay. Next he felt encumbered. Choice loomed momentous, yet cold and infinite: he could shed or not shed. An image formed in his mind. He was a snowman, impenetrable. Then he was melting. Drip, drip. Trickle, trickle. At last, his self dissipated. He believed. The Absolute was Spirit. Spirit was God. Jack Lewis was a theist.

"I give up. I admit that God is God."

Citing himself as "the most dejected and reluctant convert in all England," he wrote to Owen Barfield:

> *Terrible things are happening to me. The*
> *"Spirit". . .is showing an alarming tendency*
> *to become much more personal and is taking*
> *the offensive, and behaving just like God.*
> *You'd better come on Monday at the latest or*
> *I may have entered a monastery. . .*[3]

In August Jack unsealed an alarming letter from Uncle

Richard, who lived in Scotland but was vacationing in Belfast. Albert, felled by excruciating stomach pains, was in hospital getting x-rays. No one had to tell Jack what that could mean! Would stomach cancer claim his father as it already had his mother? Jack left for Little Lea at once.

In Belfast the doctor calmed Jack, "The obstruction in his bowel is not cancer."

Jack stayed with his father in Little Lea. The horrors surrounding the death of Mrs. Moore's brother, Doc, besieged Jack, yet were another variety. Albert was in agony, but he was sane. Worse for Jack, however, every room seemed choked with the bogies of childhood—the awful rows with his father, the dreaded returns to school, the heartbreak of a dying mother. In September, Albert was taken to the hospital again.

The doctor was contrite. "It is cancer. We'll have to operate."

"Recovering" in the hospital, Albert died at 68. To Warnie, who was in China, Jack wrote on October 27:

> *I always before condemned as sentimentalists or hypocrites the people whose view of the dead was so different from the view they held of the same people living. Now (I find) out that it is a natural process. . .A dozen times while I was making the funeral arrangements I found myself mentally jotting down some episode or other to tell him. . .By the way, a great deal of his jollity and jokes remained until the end. . .four days before his death. . .the day nurse said (to me), "I've just been telling Mr. Lewis that he's exactly like my father. . .a pessimist." (To which Father retorted), "I suppose he has several daughters" . . .As time goes on, the thing that emerges is*

> *that. . .he was a terrific personality. . .Remember*
> *(the quote): "(Samuel) Johnson is dead. Let us go*
> *on to the next. There is none.". . .How (Father)*
> *filled a room. . .(although) physically he was not*
> *a big man. . .Our whole world is either direct or*
> *indirect testimony. . .The way we enjoyed going to*
> *Little Lea, and the way we hated it, and the way*
> *we enjoyed hating it. . .And now you could do*
> *anything on earth you cared to in the study at*
> *midday on a Sunday, and it is beastly. . .*[4]

That Jack and Warnie would discuss selling Little Lea whenever Warnie could return from China seemed unbelievable. But what choice did they have? Jack was committed to Oxford. Warnie had a solid fifteen years invested in the Army. Retirement for either of them in Ireland was years away. The only benefit about the whole sad affair was Jack's reconciliation with Arthur. When he returned to Oxford, the letters began flowing back and forth again. He and Mrs. Moore even stayed as guests at Bernagh, Arthur's home, in December.

By Christmas time 1929, Jack was meeting regularly with Tolkien, whom he now affectionately called "Tollers." Usually they met Monday mornings in Jack's rooms at Magdalen. Incredibly, Tolkien had won Jack over so completely that Jack now supported Tolkien's change in curriculum. Old English and Middle English were expanded at the expense of Victorian Literature. Now the study of English Literature stopped at Keats' death in 1821.

"You may study more recent writers if you wish," Lewis would tell his pupils plainly, "but I doubt if I can spare the time to discuss them with you."

While Jack enjoyed Tolkien's friendship, he was not a first-rate dialectician like Barfield. Tolkien was too passionate; he lost his temper, which was fatal. Obviously, Jack's stringent standards for companions had mellowed. Or perhaps they had been false. Jack had never held Arthur to those standards, and Tolkien was like Arthur, with the added ingredient of genius.

Tollers related to Jack that not only was he too a product of Norse mythology and the modern mythmakers, George MacDonald and William Morris, but also that he was writing a myth for England. As Jack began to realize the scope of Tolkien's *Silmarillion*, however, he was astonished. Tolkien had created an enormous ancient world: Middle-earth. It was not alien, but the precursor of our own. Deep in antiquity, it swarmed with elves and dwarves and evil orcs. The elves fashioned three great jewels, the "Silmarilli." The jewels were stolen by the evil Morgoth. Many wars followed as the elves fought to recover them. Tolkien had even invented two languages for the elves: Quenya and Sindarin. They were languages with many hundreds of words, all meticulously fashioned from root words.

"But where is your Christ?" Jack teased gently.

"The 'One' is the Trinity in my story. The 'Valar,' the guardians of my world, are angelic beings. Only once in the story do they surrender their power to the 'One.' The Trinity, or 'One,' reigns over this ancient world, but is never seen. You see, the story is remote and strange, but it's not a lie."

Jack's own world continued to expand and change. As he read Tolstoy's *War and Peace*, he was astonished. He had always considered the novel quite inferior to narrative poetry, but Tolstoy's genius had made Jack "feel" the story, even war.

"It's very close to perfect," he raved, "and sustained for half a million words!"

Over his own writing, he agonized long and hard, considering prose as an option. Although at one time he had purposed within himself that he would do anything to get published and have a huge literary success, he did not feel that way at all now. And he was not being false. He credited it to his new-found faith in God.

In April of 1930, Warnie returned from China. Together the brothers started sifting through everything in Little Lea. Memories threatened to suffocate them. They set aside all they wanted to keep in one room. Childhood toys they buried in the back yard. The rest of the belongings were designated to be thrown away, given away, or auctioned. Warnie volunteered to request a transfer to England so that he could arrange thousands of letters and documents Albert had left behind. Knowing already that Mrs. Moore wanted Warnie to live with them, Jack invited Warnie again.

"You'll be leaving the Army in a few years," reasoned Jack. "Tell me, what better place is there to stay than with us? We can take the money from Little Lea and buy a house in Oxford."

Warnie agreed.

Later at Little Lea, when Warnie came upon Jack reading, he stopped dead in his tracks. "I say! Is that you—the angry young man of *Spirits in Bondage*—reading the Bible?"

"The New Testament in Greek. John, in fact," grinned Jack.

"The Book of John yet!" Warnie's mouth hung open.

"It will spoil the rest of my reading for some time, no doubt," Jack remarked dryly.

Warnie blinked. How did Jack mean that? But he didn't pry. He was the politest of men now.

Back in Oxford, Jack and Mrs. Moore set out to find a house. Of course it had to be east of Oxford so Jack would not have to worm his way though the town's entire conglomeration of autos and bicycles and pedestrians to reach Magdalen. In July they checked a house three miles east of Oxford on the flats below the north flank of Shotover Hill.

"Goodness!" exclaimed Jack as they were driven down a road barely more than two worn ruts. Then the car turned onto a trail even more primitive. "Are you sure you want to continue?"

"Think of the privacy," she instructed, but doubt softened her voice. " We've come this far; let's see it."

"Do I see some monstrous decrepit brick kilns through the trees?" Jack tittered.

"The house is only eight years old."

Soon they entered the property, facing the back of the house. The house, of red brick with a clay-tiled roof over a dormered second floor, appeared larger than the one they lived in. They left the car and entered the house through the back door. The main floor had two sitting rooms and two bedrooms, besides a kitchen, a pantry, and a maid's room. The second floor had three bed-rooms. Electricity was provided by a gasoline generator. All hot water had to be heated on the kitchen stove.

"We must have this house," whispered Mrs. Moore to Jack.

"Perhaps we should look at other houses," grumbled Jack as they stepped outside the front door. Then he blinked. The grounds in front of the house took his breath away.

"The grounds go all the way onto Shotover Hill, up to that belt of fir trees," pointed the man who had brought them. "Eight acres."

"No!" doubted Jack. "All the way onto Shotover Hill?" It was too good to be true. Besides the lower wooded slope of Shotover Hill, the grounds included a good-sized lawn, a tennis court, a green house, a work shed, the two enormous brick kilns, and a very large pond from an old clay pit.

"We must have it," Jack whispered now to Mrs. Moore.

The next day they brought Warnie. He too blinked in disbelief. "I can't imagine such a house and grounds being available near Oxford for three times what they are asking." He began calculating what it would cost to add two more rooms so that each brother might have his own private study.

They purchased the house. All legal work was processed by none other than Owen Barfield, who had been forced to relegate literature to a hobby. Mrs. Moore put up half the money and became the official owner. The Lewis brothers put up the other half. Mrs. Moore's will left the house to the brothers for their lifetime. After that, the house would become Maureen's.

As was so often the case, their joy was blunted by sorrow. Jack received a heartrending letter from his cousin Ruth Hamilton stating that her mother, Jack's favorite Aunt Annie, had died of cancer at sixty-four. "She so much wanted to live," grieved Ruth in her letter. Now cancer had taken Jack's mother, father, and favorite aunt.

Warnie too took it very hard. "I could take the loss of four people easier than the loss of Aunt Annie. Now I feel like Little Lea has died for good." Jack had not realized Warnie was so attached to Aunt Annie. The brothers were so close and yet hid so much from each other.

By October all but Warnie had moved into the red brick house, though Jack still lived in Magdalen much of the time. From then on their house was called the "Kilns." That same month he started to "fly the flag" for God and began to attend service in Chapel every morning.

At dinner one night, Mrs. Moore suggested widening the road into the Kilns. "But won't that require cutting down all those lovely silver birch trees?" objected Warnie, who was on a short leave from the Army.

He looked to Jack for support, but Jack said nothing. Later, Warnie, much upset, brought up the subject privately with Jack. How could he let Mrs. Moore remove all those lovely trees?

Jack smiled. "You must resist the temptation to react to domestic proposals by Mrs. Moore or Maureen. Nine out of ten are never mentioned a second time."

In January the two brothers took their own walking tour together, trekking over fifty miles along the Wye Valley. Warnie still had to learn from Jack who had learned from Arthur that one had to enjoy every outing, no matter how cold or foggy or rainy. Before long, Warnie became a congenial companion.

"This should be just the first of many 'winter' walks, Arch-Piggy-Bottom."

"Agreed, Small-Piggy-Bottom."

On their return to the Kilns, the brothers planted forty-three trees: chestnuts, ashes, oaks, and firs. Over the next few months, Jack was surprised to learn Warnie was coming to God too, most reluctantly, almost apologetically—just as he had. In Jack's mind, Warnie's idea of good was much less than his own. Warnie believed the old chestnut that it merely meant that one didn't harm other people. Warnie could attain his idea of good; Jack could not possibly achieve his ill-defined holiness. In May of 1931, Warnie openly embraced Christ, really stunning Jack. After all their years together, Jack never expected that. One Saturday, explained Warnie, he suddenly became aware life could not be an accident and began saying his prayers. He had no more explanation than that.

"This old fat tire has made a complete revolution," he illustrated for Jack. "Belief to indifference to skepticism to atheism to agnosticism to belief."

Quite often they discussed Jack's dilemma over Christ. "What holds me back," Jack expounded, "is that I cannot conceive of the immediacy of Christ. Except as an example, how can the life and death of someone who lived 2000 years ago help me here and now? I know enough about Christianity to know Christ's example is not the heart of Christianity. You must believe the blood of the Lamb atones now."

Jack further discussed his dilemma with Tolkien. One such meeting took place September 19, 1931. This meeting was not their customary one during the week; it was on Saturday. It was not in the morning; it was at night. It was not in Jack's room; it was on Addison's walk among the deer and elms. Jack and Tolkien were joined by Hugo Dyson, a professor of English at Reading University whose specialty was the late seventeenth century. Jack considered him "a fastidious book man," yet "burly, both in mind and body, with the stamp of the war on him."

Dyson was not only a Christian, but also a tireless, irrepressible needler. "You're an Old Testament Jew, Lewis."

"Perhaps, but Orthodox Jews don't crave immortality," Jack came back defensively. "Such a desire corrupts belief, because it demands belief."

"Christianity is not desirable for that reason," countered Tolkien, "or for any reason of convenience. Christianity is true, a historical fact."

"If I can't understand the meaning of the Crucifixion or of the Resurrection or of Redemption, how can I believe in Christ?" Jack expostulated.

"You love myth, don't you?" pressed Tolkien, already knowing the answer.

"Of course. Balder thrills me as much now as ever."

"So you like the element of a god dying and coming to life again?" goaded Tolkien.

"Yes," Jack granted, "but I'm not sure why."

"Indeed. Nor am I," answered Tolkien. "Why do you make such demands for clarity on Christianity? Just accept the fact that Christianity is a myth that really happened."

"But myths are lies," argued Jack, "worthless, even though they are breathed through silver and magnificent."

"No," Tolkien contended. "The myths that you consider lies are the myths of men, though they contain fragments of truth. The myth that is wholly true—the birth, death, and resurrection of Christ—is God's myth."

"Maybe I am demanding too much of the mystery," Jack conceded lamely, "but isn't belief ultimately from the grace of God?"

The following week, Jack rode in the sidecar of Warnie's motorcycle as the two brothers set out from Oxford for the wonderful new Whipsnade Zoo. It was only a trip of thirty-plus miles, but to Jack the trip spanned 2000 years. Later he could not formulate any reason or process that could explain what took place. It was as if Jack, lying long in bed, suddenly was aware he was awake because when he climbed out of that sidecar, he believed in Christ.

"God's grace," concluded a humbled Jack.

nine

Myth-Making

J ack seemed really settled now. He was a Christian, and he had a wonderful, secluded home at the Kilns. Every aspect of his life seemed better than he had ever imagined it could be. Now thirty-three, he decided that if he ever was going to be a poet of any consequence, it was high time to pursue it. And what better subject than his own conversion? He began such a story in verse, but it sputtered. Poetry seemed very difficult for him now.

"I so doubt my poetry now," he divulged to Mrs. Moore, "that I wonder if it is no more than metered prose."

Perhaps prose was his calling. He was already well under way on what he hoped would be a major academic work on the Medieval Tradition, the development of the romantic epic and no less than the evolution of the concept of love. Like Tolkien, he adored the Middle Ages. Jack was more and more defensive of the past. In November 1931, he wrote Warnie:

> *I get rather tired of the endless talk about (so-and-so) lives by his style in spite of his obsolete (theology). . .To read histories of literature, one would suppose that the great authors of the past were a sort of chorus of melodious idiots who said, in beautifully cadenced language, that black was white and that two and two made five. When one turns to the books themselves—well I, at*

*any rate, find nothing obsolete. The silly
things the great men say were silly then as
they are now; the wise ones are as wise
now as they were then. . .[1]*

Current novels were pitiful to Jack. Even when the writing was brilliant, he deemed it wasted. On one occasion he wrote Arthur that he was reading Virginia Wolfe's *Orlando* and praised her power to convey the feel of landscapes and moods, then expressed frustration with the total absence of substance on which she used her power. Above all, he loathed her cynicism, regardless that she was the darling of the modern intellectuals.

"The clevers," decried Jack contemptuously.

And so Jack willingly embraced the Middle Ages as he grappled with his work on the Medieval Tradition and the development of the romantic epic. The Middle Ages were the height of Christendom, the height of chivalry, really the height of love. Jack thought long and hard how to know the glorious fruits of the Middle Ages. First, one had to know the soil that spawned the Middle Ages. A solid knowledge of the Bible was so significant that without it, the task was hopeless. Almost as important in the fertile soil were the classic Latin and Greek works, especially Plato and Aristotle. To reap the bounty of the Middle Ages was to understand allegory and how it worked in the hands of masters. Certainly one could not ignore the English authors Chaucer, Langland, and Spenser. Two specific works of the age were paramount: the French classic, *Romance of the Rose*, and Dante's allegory, *The Divine Comedy*. In Jack's mind, *The Divine Comedy* was the greatest single achievement by one man in literature. It was the culmination of the wisdom of the Middle Ages.

Jack knew his work on Medieval Tradition would take several years, but as he grappled with the concept of allegory, the idea for a book about his conversion solidified. Allegory was not popular with moderns. Even Tolkien bristled at the suggestion that his *Silmarillion* was allegory. Jack was convinced, however, that in the hands of a master an allegory could reveal truth that could not be revealed as well by any other method. Well-contrived allegory approached myth in power, but had to be understood with the imagination instead of intellect. As Jack pondered the most effective context of his conversion as an allegory, he naturally associated it—since both were quests for salvation—with John Bunyan's great seventeenth century allegory, *Pilgrim's Progress*. Sporadically Jack would think on it, allowing the idea to ferment for a while. Although the thought that he again had picked a literary form unpopular with moderns flitted through his mind, it didn't bother him.

"Good heavens," he bantered with Tolkien, "the last thing you or I would ever want to do would be to write a 'popular' book like the 'clevers.'"

Meanwhile Warnie had been reassigned to China, stationed again in Shanghai. Perhaps he wouldn't get out of the Army so soon after all. Jack's life, to the contrary, continued in full flourish. He embarked on his usual walking tour in 1932 with his friends. The outing was not so contentious now that Jack was a Christian, but they still found plenty about which to needle each other. As far as the outdoors was concerned, Jack perceived it all as colors and smells and sounds and moods. Only occasionally did he know the name of a plant or a rock. Nor did he care, for to him the name conveyed next to nothing. A scientific name was nothing but two Latin words, forever pitifully enslaved.

After one excursion he wrote Warnie:

Wallaby Wood. . .(had) masses of bluebells;
the graceful, fawn-like creatures hopping out
of one pool of sunshine into another over
English wildflowers. . .and English wild birds
singing deafeningly all round, came nearer to
one's idea of the world before the Fall than
anything I ever hoped to see. . .[2]

But 1932 became unusually burdensome for Jack. By the end of July, he noted that because of sickness, tutoring, lecturing, and academic writing, he had not enjoyed one morning with a book for eighteen weeks! Certainly he had not written any account of his spiritual conversion. "This has been the driest spell of my adult life," he lamented. He could hardly wait for the August vacation he had planned with Arthur.

Upon reaching Arthur's home, "Bernagh," in Ireland, he attacked the writing of his conversion in a frenzy. "Pen! Ink!" he bellowed as he launched the allegory of his quest for salvation. Jack's pilgrim John, taught to fear the Landlord of his native country Puritania, visualizes an island, Joy, and sets off to find it. After many false destinations, John finds his way back to Puritania, the symbol of his mother church, and salvation. Because the hero finds salvation by retracing his steps to Puritania, Jack titled the book *Pilgrim's Regress*. By the time he departed Ireland, it was finished.

The feat of writing such a work in two weeks stunned Jack as much as anyone. Prose gushed forth from him, and revisions were minor. Nonetheless, writing prose was not mere words. It was a creation, a mass of ideas. Suddenly, it was clear to Jack that he had a gift for writing prose. Writing verse was torture in comparison. And who could say one form was better than another? In fact, he detested modern poetry, not only because of its free verse, but because it embraced atheism and Marxism. Even T.S. Eliot, a professed Christian, was barely tolerable to Jack. Eliot created metaphors that were ludicrous to Jack. "Pure bosh!" Jack would rant.

"Besides that, Eliot is an insufferable elitist," he fustigated to Mrs. Moore.

J.M. Dent, who had published *Dymer*, liked Jack's prose well enough to accept *Pilgrim's Regress* and schedule it to be released in the summer of 1933. Because the Japanese attacked China in 1932, and the situation was rapidly deteriorating, Warnie applied for retirement from the army and left China. By Christmas of 1932, he was back in England—a civilian, and resident of the Kilns. Because the two-room "wing" had recently been completed, the two brothers had their own studies.

That winter dumped the worst snowstorm in thirty years on Oxford—the snow drifted into eye-level dunes. Although Jack lay in bed with a cold, he truly relished the "ordinary" sickness. After trying to keep apace with an unrelenting and tiring schedule, nothing afforded more delight than a concrete reason to stay in bed. Of course, he was never too indisposed to read, especially *Phantastes*, which was practically his devotional.

At Oxford, the Kolbitars had read all the Icelandic sagas and the group had evaporated, but Tolkien and Jack were too close now not to meet and share their writings. Together they joined an undergraduate writing club hosted by Edward Tangye Lean called the Inklings. When Lean graduated in June of 1933 and the Inklings, as an undergraduate club, died, Jack adopted the name for the meetings he was already holding for his colleagues once a week in his rooms at Magdalen. No records or minutes were kept. The sole purpose of the meetings was providing a forum for the Inklings to read their writings to one another. Because Jack was a firm believer in William Blake's maxim, "Opposition is true friendship," the criticism was friendly but severe. The new group was powerful: Owen Barfield, Nevill Coghill, Hugo Dyson, and, of course, Lewis and Tolkien. All A's.

"Anything new tonight?" Jack would invite. "How about that new story of yours, Tollers? The one you call 'Hobbits.'"

Jack befriended Tolkien as closely as the latter allowed and, at times, bent to his influence. For instance, when Tolkien decided it was high time to buy a used car, Jack purchased a used car for the Kilns. Like Tolkien, he had bicycled and ridden busses for many years.

The two men reinforced each other's total rejection of dandyism, although the reed-thin Tolkien couldn't match the shabbiness of Jack, who was now pear-shaped. They wore rumpled tweed jackets and baggy flannel pants. Although essential, their ties appeared to be afterthoughts. Shoes were heavy clogs, suitable for walking trips. Never one to avoid inclement weather—walking in rain and snow must be enjoyed as one of God's more questionable delights—Jack simply added a mud-colored raincoat and a much-abused hat.

(Once along Addison's Walk, Jack retrieved a shapeless piece of fabric snagged on a branch. "Look here," he yelped, "it's the hat I lost. What luck!" Immediately he donned his ragged old friend.)

Meanwhile the Kilns had taken on a more permanent look. The staff consisted of a maid and a rough handyman from the countryside, Fred Paxford. He was the gardener, the grocery shopper, and the chauffeur, for although Jack had paid for the car, only Paxford and Maureen drove it.

Paxford knew how to pinch a penny. He was as focused as a surgeon as he took inventory of the larder, then purchased the tiniest amount of groceries that would suffice. He was loyal and honest and exasperatingly opinionated. Inwardly he was an optimist, but outwardly he was a pessimist.

"Them cabbages should be ripe now," he would announce just before working in the garden, "though I shouldn't wonder if I can't find any. If I do, the cook won't use them. And if she does, like as not, the menfolk won't eat them with their boiled beef."

Fred Paxford irritated no one but Warnie with his homespun pessimism. Warnie, retired after eighteen years of the Army, quickly decided he would not even attempt to manage the Kilns while Jack toiled in Oxford. Mrs. Moore and Fred Paxford were already doing that in tandem. Instead, Warnie gradually transferred all his papers and most of his books to Jack's small sitting room in Magdalen. Each morning he would arrive to catalog the "Lewis Papers." Quietly fixing tea, he even became a regular among the Inklings, though he only occasionally commented. Warnie had mastered the art of being polite and unobtrusive.

One friend remarked to Jack, "Warnie is the most courteous, tactful man I ever met. His politeness and total lack of selfishness seem completely natural to him—as instinctive as breathing." Jack was pleased with his friends' acceptance of Warnie.

Jack was as amazed as everyone else to learn Warnie was planning a book on the history of seventeenth century France. Warnie? A scholar, yes, but an author?

Maureen, now twenty-five and boarding at a music school in Monmouth, was at the Kilns less and less. Sunday evenings Warnie played his Beethoven records for Jack and Mrs. Moore. Jack preferred to hear complete symphonies rather than excerpts as he once had. (He applied the same logic to books.) Of course, he had strong opinions. The movement he liked best was the Seventh's third, although the finale ruined the Seventh as a whole for him. The Fifth was the best symphony overall, he acknowledged, reluctantly siding with nearly everyone else in the world, but he went against the grain in completely dis-liking the Third Symphony-Eroica. Perhaps it was because Beethoven had dedicated it to Napoleon.

"Quite frankly," he expressed to Warnie, "Napoleon reminds me of Adolph Hitler." Hitler was a demonic German who claimed by persecuting Jews he was doing the will of God. His claims were stupid but not amusing. Now the chancellor of Germany, he was freshly granted dictatorial powers. He spoke of re-arming Germany, and all opposition was consigned to concentration camps. All over Germany, Italy, Austria, Japan, and Russia—the very countries that might form an alliance around the devilish Hitler—voices of moderation were being assassinated. War loomed on the horizon. Oxford no longer felt as safe as Switzerland.

"Life goes on," shrugged Jack. "I blocked the Great War out of my mind back in 1917. I won't let this one consume my time. Not until it happens."

Surreptitiously, however, Hitler and the Italian dictator Mussolini crept into Jack's "King of Drum" narrative poem, which now bore the name, "Queen of Drum." His king is a doddering ancient. The queen is young and wild, roaming at night. The archbishop looks the other way. Seizing the day, a general takes over the kingdom! As dictator, he demands the loyalty of the queen and the archbishop. No longer can they evade the responsibilities of the kingdom.

Without affecting the flow of the narrative, Jack varied the meter of "Queen of Drum," moving back and forth between dialogue and description more skillfully than ever before.

He molded each of his five main characters distinctly, each identifiable from its speech alone. Remembering Barfield's complaint about his earlier poetry, he meticulously polished it. The creation of the poem was difficult to the point of being painful.

On May 21, 1936, Clarendon Press of the Oxford University Press published Jack's *Allegory of Love*, his scholarly work subtitled "A Study in Medieval Tradition." One of his own stated objectives was to trace the 1200-year history of Christian allegory from its birth in the Latin Prudentius to the Medieval masterpiece, *Faerie Queene* by Spenser in the late 1500s. A second objective was to trace through time the romantic conception of love. On June 6, the Literary Supplement of the *London Times*, Jack's "TLS," stated in a very detailed 2000-word review:

> *(the book is). . .scholarly, fascinating, and original. . .Mr. Lewis is both interested and skilled in the history of human psychology. He is obviously qualified to write literary history of the best kind; for his book is an example of it. . .*

One month later in America the *New York Times* reviewed *Allegory of Love:*

> *At first glance one might not imagine that there was anything more than an antiquarian interest in a subject such as the allegorical love poetry of the Middle Ages. . .But C.S. Lewis shows that it is as impossible to extricate ourselves from our literary progenitors as from our physical forebearers, and that such a form as the medieval allegory of love*

> *was not only born of the thought and cus-*
> *toms of a particular era of history, but*
> *bequeathed an important legacy to the future*
> *and finds its reflection in some of the out-*
> *standing works of our own literature. . .*

The *Spectator* indirectly admitted the difficulty of what Jack achieved:

> *The book is learned, witty and sensible, and*
> *makes one ashamed of not having read its*
> *material; in the first flush of admiration for*
> *the Romance of the Rose, I tried to read the*
> *Chaucerian version. . .But it is. . .far better*
> *to read Mr. Lewis and his admirable quota-*
> *tions. . .and frankly admit that there are*
> *great pleasures not our own. . .*

No one was more pleased than Warnie. "You've moved beyond Oxford, Jack. Even in America, it is being hailed as a major work."

Jack's life was altered. As far as being popular with the general public, he was an unknown, but he was certainly more now than a mere intimidating presence known on the sprawling campus of Oxford. He was now becoming known to English scholars all over the world. Although he shunned such accolades, many newspapers and magazines were acknowledging him as *the* expert on Medieval Literature.

One of his new admirers was Charles Williams, an editor with Oxford University Press in London. The coincidence was remarkable because Nevill Coghill had just persuaded Jack to read Williams' novel, *The Place of the Lion*, a very sophisticated and deeply religious thriller. The heroine, who studies angels and demons in academic smugness, is lured into the supernatural world. The book illuminated humility for Jack as never before.

He bewailed to Tolkien, "Tell me, Tollers! *The Place of the Lion* is one of the few Christian fantasies being written. When are we two going to sally forth?"

In 1936, upon Arthur's urging, Jack read *Voyage to Arcturus* by David Lindsay. The book, published 16 years before, was a haunting spiritual journey, much like George MacDonald's *Lilith* or *Phantastes*, except that it was more diabolical than holy. Jack was stunned. Lindsay had shown him that what George MacDonald had done—even what Charles Williams had done—could be done in space fiction. To prick even more Jack's desire to write such a fantasy was a remark by an undergraduate praising the future opportunity for man to colonize the planets. Jack found that thought revolting, knowing the kind of men who would lead such an effort.

He accosted Tolkien, "You create your myth—that tiny splinter of Christianity, the great Truth—in the distant past, influenced by the Icelandic sagas. Perhaps I can create my myth in the future."

Influenced by what? Believing the Middle Ages the epitome of Christendom and decency, Jack would use the "Medieval Model" for his myth-making in the future. For Jack the "Model" was the very comforting amalgamation of Christianity, Platonism, Aristotleism, Stoicism, and least of all, paganisms other than Latin and Greek. Of course, Christianity would always overrule the other elements in the event of conflict. This amalgamation of elements had influenced some of the greatest writers in the world: Augustine, Dante, and Spenser. Because it had held its appeal long after the Medieval Age, it had affected even

Shakespeare, Donne, and Milton.

"It's absolutely the most satisfying and most harmonious 'world view' in the history of mankind," insisted Jack to Warnie.

The Model indicated that although the universe is infinite, everything is not relative. Up is up, and down is down. The earth is the center of this universe of Ptolemy, but nonetheless a sphere. At the center of earth is hell. Therefore in the Medieval Model, earth not only represents the center of the universe and all existence, but the lowest of all existence!

Surrounding earth are nine concentric "celestial spheres," sometimes called "wheels." Moving within the spheres are the moon, the sun, and various planets. They all have attributes. The moon is dangerous; the sun is beneficial. Venus represents love and beauty. Mars represents belligerence. Giant Jupiter, the best planet, symbolizes serenity, magnanimity, and cheerfulness. Saturn, the worst, embodies aging, sickness, disease, and treachery. The eighth sphere carries the stars with their various constellations signifying different things. The Primum Mobile, or First Cause, of the ninth sphere carries no bodies but imparts the movement that pushes the bodies on all the inner spheres. Beyond that is the "Tenth Heaven, absolute reality and empyrean." It has no movement, no duration, but is eternal and infinite. Each sphere produces a perfect tone. "The harmonics are called the 'music of the spheres,' " Jack explained to Warnie.

The Medieval Model honored the Trinity. God is not the Jewish God, immediate, passionate, and terrifying. God is remote. His immensity is explained by Dante; it is the paradox of increasing space as one enters inner circles. God is a point, yet more immense than anything! The immediate God of the Trinity is Christ. All-pervasive among Christians is the Holy Spirit. Created spirits are well-detailed by

Medievalists. Each of three hierarchies consist of three species. The hierarchy uppermost and facing God consists of seraphim, cherubim, and thrones. The next, still facing God, has dominions, powers, and virtues. The lowest hierarchy are messengers: principalities (or princes), archangels, and angels. "And angels are greater than men," annotated Jack. "The Model puts us in our place."

Several levels of created material essences also exist in the Medieval Model. Lowest is all nonliving matter. Next is living matter without senses: plants. Another is living, with the five senses, but without power to reason: animals. Then highest among all created material beings is man. Mankind can reason. Reason governs the five wits: common sense, memory, imagination, fantasy, and instinct. The wits are supposed to control animal appetites or passion. Thus moral conflict is a conflict between reason and passion. On the one hand, mankind is given dominion over all living things. On the other hand, mankind is under the dominion of God, but accepts the rule of monarchs.

"But as any Medievalist knows," Jack babbled to Warnie with great relish, "yet another kind of material being with senses and the power of reason lives on earth and in the air. The *longaevi*."

The *longaevi*, though not immortal, live long lives. They are not under mankind's dominion. Capable of being good or evil, the assemblage includes pans, elves, giants, goblins, fairies, nymphs, dwarfs, and other *longaevi* who avoid men. In Jack's mind, for mankind has not always agreed on whether *longaevi* are to be feared or enjoyed, they softened the classic severity of the grand design, despite their slight rebellion.

He set his perspective to verse for Tolkien's ancient myth:

There was a time before the ancient sun
And swinging wheels of heaven had learned
to run
More certainly than dreams; for dreams them-
selves
Had bodies then and filled the world with elves.
The starveling lusts whose walk is now con-
fined
To darkness and the cellarage of the mind,
And shudderings and despairs and shapes of sin
Then walked at large and were not cooped
within.
Though cast a shadow; brutes could speak:
and men
Get children on a star. For spirit then
Threaded a fluid world and dreamed it new
Each moment. Nothing was false or new.[3]

Of course, Jack did not believe the Model literally. The Model was but an image for myth-making.

"But in fact," wondered Warnie, "how will you use the model to create a myth of the future for space fiction?"

ten

"No one can write space fiction in which the planets orbit around earth in these days," Warnie cautioned.

"I'm only using a geocentric universe metaphorically," defended Jack.

Images that preceded all of Jack's fiction constantly bubbled in his mind. Sometimes he felt no urge to put them into some form, and sometimes he did. This time he most certainly did, yet the effervescence nagged him, disturbing his work, his meals, his sleep. He knew Earth had to be the hellish planet. He finally determined to use the scientifically-known arrangement of the solar system but follow his own image of space, inspired by the Medieval Model. Planets are not merely islands with possible life in the void of space. Space itself is alive, tingling. The planets are holes in God's living heaven.

In Jack's space fiction, Maleldil is the Christ-like one of the Trinity. Maleldil is spirit, but also being and immanent. Maleldil's father is the remote God, who is terrifying. This awesome God is not vague because he is indefinite, but vague because man can't describe such concreteness. God is light, landscape, beauty.

Each planet is ruled by an angelic being called oyarsa. Oyarsas are roughly equivalent to principalities (or princes). They are not infinitely wise, but are angels far superior to men. Under them are eldils. All these spiritual beings move about freely in the Field of Arbol (the living space) and speak Old Solar. Lesser beings—not spirit but material—have their own languages. To celebrate, the spiritual beings all participate in the Great Dance—the harmony of the spheres.

The earth is unique. Its oyarsa—the Bent One—rebels. His evil is moral evil. Because God permits natural evil, as in animals, but not moral evil, earth becomes isolated, the "Silent Planet." Old Solar is completely lost. The Bent One has already attacked the moon and Mars—the latter the location of Jack's novel. The outer surface of Mars is a dead wasteland, but on a deeper level live three kinds of material beings.

And so Jack wrote his space adventure called *Out of the Silent Planet.* An evil scientist, Weston, wants to "conquer" space. He kidnaps the hero Ransom and takes him to Malacandra (Mars) because he thinks the rulers there want a sacrifice. Instead, Ransom escapes and makes friends with the three kinds of material beings that live on Mars. The inhabitants are universally obedient and uncorrupted because they have no free will. Finally Weston is subdued by the oyarsa and sent back to earth with Ransom.

"Saving both Weston and Ransom hints of a sequel," observed Warnie.

Publishers, unimpressed with *Out of the Silent Planet*, doubted that it would be commercial. Influenced by hard science fiction with its gadgets, they scoffed at Jack's metaphysics. With Tolkien's help, however, Jack finally secured a publisher, Bodley Head. In general, the book was warmly reviewed after it was released in 1938, even though reviewers recognized that the writing and sophisticated metaphysics were vastly superior to most space fiction. In Jack's fiction, the underlying Christianity was far more apparent than in Tolkien's.

"Yet only two of sixty reviewers figured out the Bent One was the devil!" marveled Jack. "It's quite obvious any amount of theology can be smuggled into people's minds under the cover of an adventure story without them knowing it."

He wasn't pleased with the alarming self-centered humanism of the times that the statistics revealed. "But," he excused the reviewers to himself, "my book is quite trivial compared to world events." In fact, Hitler's Germany was getting one concession after another in Europe. Sometime the concessions would have to stop. War seemed certain. How he hated the news!

"Why should such quiet ruminants like you and I have been born in such a ghastly age?" Jack demanded of Warnie. Warnie was forty-three; Jack, almost forty. Both were pear-shaped and balding.

That same year, 1938, John Masefield, now Poet Laureate of England, contacted Jack. "At our playhouse in August, we would like a fresh narrative poem presented by a poet skilled at reading. Nevill Coghill tells me you are a prime candidate."

"I have a poem I call *Queen of Drum*," Jack offered.

"Excellent. Perhaps I could preview it."

When Masefield met with Jack after reading the poem, he was enthusiastic. He had read it twice. The last canto about the queen escaping into Fairyland he considered extraordinary. It rushed to its end breathlessly:

> *And all the world was falling,*
> *Spirit and soul were falling,*
> *Body, brain and heart*
> *Vanishing, falling apart;*
> *Vacancy under vacancy*

Shuddering gaped below;
"Go," was her prayer, "Go,
Go away, go away, away from me."
And the fear heightened,
The command tautened;
Between her spirit and soul, dividing,
The razor-edged, ice-brook cold command
  was gliding,
Till suddenly, at the worst, all changed,
And like a thing far off, estranged,
Only remembered, like a mood,
The dread became. Her mortal blood
Flowed freely in the uncolored calm,
Which woos despair and is its balm.
Nothing now she will ever want again
But to glide out of the world of men,
Nor will she turn to right or left her head,
But go straight on. She has tasted elven
  bread.
And so the story tells, she passed away
Out of the world: but if she dreams to-day
In fairy land, or if she wakes in Hell,
(The chance being one in ten), it doesn't tell.[1]

Masefield pointed out that the length presented a problem for a dramatic reading. The poem was enormous now: five cantos totaled 1500 lines. A reading would consume nearly two hours. Could Jack read only the first and last cantos? Jack consented, but he felt like with this last discombobulated reading he was burying his narrative poetry. The genre was appreciated by few moderns, who rather savored self-absorbed, introspective humanistic poetry. That repelled Jack. Disappointingly, Jack's classic rhymes and meters were

127

also unappreciated. As if to rub one last measure of salt into the wound, *Queen of Drum* had been exceedingly difficult to compose.

"I can write prose a hundred times faster, and it is read by a hundred times as many people," he stormed to Warnie.

"I believe then that your prose enjoys a 10,000: one advantage, brother," Warnie calculated.

By early 1939, Jack confided in Owen Barfield that he was almost totally convinced he had no future in poetry. He didn't have to mention how freely his prose works flowed. At that time, Oxford University Press had just published a book written jointly by Jack and E.M.W. Tillyard, a literary critic at Cambridge University. They had taken opposing views of a subject that was one of Jack's pet peeves. Jack argued very strongly that to critique an artist's work by studying his life was not valid. If the artist was truly objective about his work, his own personality could not be discerned in the work. Jack believed that with all his heart. Many writers did. Moreover, the new criticism seemed a form of titillation, a sleazy peek into an artist's private life. To Jack, who liked to compartmentalize his life and cherished privacy, the whole approach was offensive.

Also in 1939, Oxford University Press published a collection of Jack's essays called *Rehabilitations*. He regarded their only common theme to be "a certain belief about life and books." One of the nine essays was a defense of ancient English poetry which used alliteration—the repetition of consonants—as the primary poetic device. W.H. Auden and Tolkien were fond of alliteration too. Jack used his own poem "Planets"—choked with Medieval meaning—to illustrate. A portion on Jupiter read:

> . . .*Of wrath ended*
> *And woes mended, of winter passed*
> *And guilt forgiven, and good fortune*
> *Jove is master; and jocund revel,*
> *Laughter of ladies. The lion-hearted,*
> *The myriad-minded, men like the gods,*
> *Helps and heroes, helms of nations*
> *Just and gentle, are Jove's children,*
> *Work his wonders. On his wide forehead*
> *Calm and kingly, no care darkens*
> *Nor wrath wrinkles; but righteous power*
> *And leisure and largess their loose splendors*
> *Have wrapped around him—a rich mantle*
> *of ease and empire. . .*[2]

Reviewers began to voice their awe at Jack's ability to ill-minate any subject. The review of *Rehabilitations* in *Books* stated:

> *Mr. Lewis' thinking is of the kind that plays*
> *over any topic with lightness and quick appre-*
> *hensions. . .(He) has a genius for careful dis-*
> *tinctions that will bear long pondering. . .*

The *Manchester Guardian* echoed the praise:

> *Learning and life, scholarship and raciness,*
> *are not easily or often combined. But Mr.*
> *Lewis does it. No one reading these essays,*
> *all of which were originally delivered as*
> *addresses to various societies, can doubt the*
> *range or precision of his learning. But it is*
> *always in close touch with the simple essen-*
> *tials of human experience which it clarifies,*
> *and from which it derives its savor. . .*

That same year of 1939, Jack was approached by Ashley Sampson, whose Geoffrey Bles Publishing ran a series of books called "Christian Challenge." Would Jack write a 40,000-word book on "the problem of pain"? His treatise would be the essential defense or "apology" to the atheist's favorite proposition: "If God were good, He would want his creatures to be happy. If God were all powerful, He would see that they were. But they are not all happy. Therefore, He lacks goodness or power or both!" Implied in the question was that God didn't exist at all.

How familiar to Jack were all the stock arguments against God! Who had used them more relentlessly than he had before 1929? And hadn't he been battered down over thousands of hours by the likes of Barfield and Harwood and Tolkien? So he accepted the assignment. This challenge would add one more aspect of writing to his growing repertoire: his defense of Christianity, or "apologetics," written not for the scholar but for the layman.

To Warnie he expounded, "I must convince the reader that I advocate Christianity not because I like it or that I think it is good for society, but because it is true. It happened. It is the central fact of our existence! And the apology must be in the common language of the people, just as the Gospel was. If an ivory-tower type like me cannot express my apologetics in common language, it indicates one of two things: Either I do not understand what I am writing about or I don't really believe it myself. This book is no small charge. Convincing a reader of an idea is like driving a sheep down a road. If any gate is open to the left or right, the reader will certainly dart into it, and the idea will be forgotten."

As a Christian, Jack was only about ten years old. How could he be so certain about Christianity? How did he have such ready answers not only to all the old chestnuts but to difficult impromptu questions? He was certain because he felt as G.K. Chesterton had felt. Christianity is true and real and historical. Thus, no matter from what angle you approach it, it is reality.

In August of 1939, Warnie reported to Jack, "Russia has signed a 'peace' pact with Germany and backed off to watch. The countries to the east, between Germany and Russia, are ripe for the German harvest. Unfortunately, one of them is Poland. We Brits are obligated to defend Poland. War for us is inevitable, Jack."

Life changed for everyone in England. The very next month, Warnie—as an army reservist—was called to duty in Yorkshire. Jack enlisted in the Home Guard and volunteered to be a religious lecturer to airmen and officers in the Royal Air Force. Because it seemed London would be bombed by the Germans, most children were evacuated. The rest of England took them in. The Kilns was no exception. Mrs. Moore welcomed several schoolgirls. Then, as everyone expected, Germany invaded Poland, and England and France declared war on Germany. By October Warnie was sent with British troops to France.

Jack was invited to give a sermon to the faculty and undergraduates at Oxford's historic Church of St. Mary the Virgin. He felt humbled as he climbed the same spiraling stairway to the same pulpit that had featured John Wesley and other great spiritual leaders. Personal emotions, however, provided no excuse to shirk responsibility. Jack's mission was no less than to explain to the undergraduates why they must pursue their education with all diligence, even though the war was very likely to drag them away, even though they might never return. "Fear must not deter us from doing our very best for the glory of God," he adjured.

Jack, who had suffered the trenches of a war, spoke with the advantage of first-hand experience, but he quickly discovered that lecturing airmen around England was far different than speaking to fellow scholars in a hard-fought, well-known vernacular. Understandably, these laymen had their own vernacular, and it was no less valid than that of the scholars, but Jack had to adjust to the fact that many terms understood among scholars to mean a specific thing meant something else to the laymen. To the laymen, "church" meant a sacred building, not a body of followers in Christ. "Charity" meant alms for the poor, not Christian love. "Dogma" was some unproved assertion presented in an arrogant manner. "Crucifixion" did not convey an execution preceded by agonizing torture; its familiarity had made it a painless, sanitized ritual. "Primitive Christianity" was not at all to the laymen the wonderful, pure Christianity practiced by the Apostles. No, it meant something backward, crude, and unfinished!

"Defining every term is self-defeating," Jack discussed with Tolkien. "Nothing can be done unless we move completely away from this language of the scholars and the clergy. Apologetics has to be driven by the simplest words in the English language." Jack was intrigued by the fact that, two hundred years before, John Wesley had ventured away from Oxford to evangelize with those identical conclusions about language.

While Jack's teaching load was wilting as undergraduates went to war, his mind was teeming with ideas for books. Besides *The Problem of Pain,* he had a sequel to *Out of the Silent Planet* and a satire about devils in mind. The war in Europe was a disaster. Germany had run the British army, including Warnie, right off the continent. By August of 1940, Warnie was put in the Army reserve and allowed to return to Oxford.

That same month Maureen married Leonard Blake, the

musical director at Worksop College in the county of Nottingham many miles north of Oxford.

Now both brothers served in the Home Guard, lugging a rifle around the dark streets of Oxford one night every week or so. Both also attended the meetings of the Inklings on Thursday nights. Charles Williams, now working in Oxford because the Oxford University Press had closed his London office, had joined the Inklings. Jack had never met anyone with a physical presence like Williams: he exuded holiness. Not only Jack felt that way. W.H. Auden and T.S. Eliot, men not easily impressed, were dumbfounded by the same feeling about Williams. Auden began touting Williams as the mentor of his later verse. On the other hand, Eliot began claiming Williams as his protégé.

In 1940 Williams, fifty-four, was so highly regarded in literary circles, he was allowed to lecture at Oxford even though he lacked a college degree. Of one lecture that Jack himself attended, he wrote:

> . . .*here was a man who really cared with every fiber of his being about "the sage and serious doctrine of virginity" which would never occur to the ordinary modern critic to take seriously. . .It was a beautiful sight to see a whole roomful of modern young men and women sitting in that absolute silence which cannot be faked. . .spellbound. . .*[3]

He added something else, more for himself than for Williams:

> . . .*I wonder, is it the case that the man who has the audacity to get up in any corrupt*

133

> *society and squarely preach justice or valor*
> *or the like always wins?. . .*[4]

Jack and Charles Williams became great friends, without regard to the fact that they were not uncritical of each other's work. Jack thought Williams was undisciplined, and that once in a while this fault exploded into poor taste. Conjuring up a romance between Mary Magdalene and John the Baptist, as Williams did in one work, grated on Jack like chalk squawking on a blackboard, yet he admired Williams' incredible imagination, the most fertile Jack had ever been around. Williams erupted with original ideas. He was electric. Like Jack, he could astonish even other scholars by quoting long passages from memory.

Williams urged Jack to take more chances with his writing, yet, on the other hand, he continually expressed awe both of Jack's mastery of the classics and of his unparalleled ability to assess literature. Williams had met those who had attempted lofty conversations, but none had possessed the vigor and joy the Inklings, especially Jack, displayed.

"You know, Jack," he complimented, "my wife didn't like it here and went back to London. And I couldn't bear it here myself, except for you. . .and the Inklings, of course."

In October of that same year, Geoffrey Bles published Jack's *The Problem of Pain*. Scholars ignored it, but since its plain, everyday language was aimed at the layman anyway, from that standpoint it was an immediate success. The book had to be reprinted twice that year, and sales did not slack off the following year.

"Its sole purpose is to explain suffering," maintained Jack. "Most pain in men is inflicted by other men, perhaps even Satan. Yet," Jack yielded, "some pain must be attributed to God. Why would God make men suffer? The hard answer is that in no ways other than pain and death can God make man surrender his self to God. 'Happy' people ignore God; 'unhappy' people seek God and desire the peace and security of his Kingdom." Thus Jack explained why an all-powerful, loving God permits pain. Jack even dealt with pain in animals, a fact many moderns find more intolerable than pain in humans.

Warnie praised the book. "It really explains the basic Christian doctrines and is helpful to the Christian in fending off the most common criticisms of Christianity. To be certain, it's helpful to all Englishmen in this time of great agony."

The book did indeed deal with far more than "the problem of pain." In it, Jack described the Fall of Man and his elemental wickedness, which moderns prefer not to acknowledge whatsoever. He explained heaven and hell. He addressed the phenomenon of the "numinous" and discussed the awe, even dread, we feel for the supernatural. He extolled the nature of God and His love for us. He emphasized the love God expects from us. He examined all the doctrines modern man finds so difficult to accept. All these were the doctrines that the liberal clergy, unable to explain, were abandoning.

In May of 1941, Jack began writing weekly installments of satire for the *Guardian*, a weekly newspaper of the Church of England. Each segment was a letter from the retired devil, Screwtape, to his young pupil, Wormwood, who was tempting his first human. The first letter to Wormwood detailed how to undermine the victim's faith in prayer. Each subsequent letter took up another way to tempt and trip and snare, and each was devilishly witty. Eventually Jack wrote thirty-one letters, enough to compile a book.

"Geoffrey Bles wants to publish the Screwtape letters as a book," Jack conferred with Warnie, "but it doesn't seem right for me to make money off evangelizing."

Already Jack was evangelizing on another front. The director of religious broadcasting for the British Broadcasting Corporation was so impressed by the lucidity of *The Problem of Pain* that he asked Jack to speak on "BBC" radio. Jack detested the radio, yet agreed because thousands might hear him. He knew exactly what he wanted to say. The New Testament assumed men understood God's natural law and knew when they were wicked. All ancient men, even pagans, knew right and wrong; modern men were ignorant. They had to be instructed in God's natural law before they were ready for the fruits of Christianity. Jack produced a series of four talks billed as "Right and Wrong."

He spoke at a deliberate, slow, conversational pace of about 150 words per minute. Listening to the recordings, he was surprised how the slow delivery had heightened his Oxfordian accent. The radio consultants, however, pronounced his baritone voice as superb for radio: it was articulate, lucid, and resonant. His talks were so well received, he was later informed, that he was talking not to thousands but hundreds of thousands!

The Royal Air Force now solicited him to specifically instruct airmen in basic Christianity. Any reluctance he might have felt about surrendering more of his time dissipated when he visited the air base in Norfolk. The crews were flying into Europe on night bombing raids.

"The airmen have a tour of duty that lasts thirty missions," stated the chaplain.

"They must be very relieved when their tour is completed," sympathized Jack.

"On the average," the chaplain paused, "a man lasts only

thirteen missions. . ."

Jack was stunned. "Then they are most likely doomed!"

"Yes." The chaplain's voice had gone flat.

"No one needs Christ more than these men do."

When Jack was urged also to continue his broadcasts, he began another series of radio talks in the same vein called "What Christians Believe." He had less and less time now for his former activities. To make matters more difficult, he and Warnie had to sell their car. Gasoline was too hard to obtain. Once again, the brothers rode a double-decker bus to and from Oxford. Still, in Jack's spare moments, he managed to write. As his radio talks made him more well known around England, he began receiving hundreds of letters. He answered every one.

The Screwtape Letters was published in February of 1942. Jack had by this time resolved his guilt over profiting from religious writing. The money from any of his religious works from then on was donated to charity. He dedicated *The Screwtape Letters* to Tolkien. Previous books had been dedicated to Hugo Dyson, the Inklings, and Warnie. No friend needed to be concerned about being left out at the rate Jack was publishing his prose.

"Nor does any friend need worry about my dedication making them a household name," joked Jack. "My books aren't widely read. They aren't exactly bestsellers."

"I wonder what kind of reception *The Screwtape Letters* will get?" Warnie mused aloud.

Jack sighed. "A smattering of interest, I suppose."

eleven

"*T*he *London Times* has reviewed *Screwtape*, Jack," announced Warnie ominously on the morning of February 28, 1942. He handed Jack the newspaper.

"First review we've seen, isn't it?" inquired Jack indifferently.

But Jack was very interested in how "TLS," the Literary Supplement of the *London Times*, would review *The Screwtape Letters*. He read:

> *On the whole the book is brilliantly success-ful. A reviewer's task is not to be a prophet, and time alone can show whether it is or is not an enduring piece of satirical writing... It is much more to the point that in so read-able a fashion Mr. Lewis has contrived to say much that a distracted world greatly requires to hear...*

So TLS was hinting the book might be enduring. Only time would tell. The *Manchester Guardian* was not so cautious:

> *...in a book of any length, satire easily top-ples over into farce and any levity in the treat-ment of such a subject would be fatal. Mr. Lewis never fails. The book is sparkling yet*

*truly reverent, in fact a perfect joy, and should
become a classic. . .*

A classic! Jack had to brush off such praise. It was dangerous. Praise in other reviews, however, was unstinting as well. The first printing of *The Screwtape Letters* sold out before publication because of its following in the *Guardian*. The book soon merited a life of its own. It was reprinted eight times in the first year! "C.S. Lewis" was now truly a national figure.

"You'll soon be well known all over the English-speaking world, I suppose," flattered Warnie.

"That's horrifying," squawked Jack. "What if the letters increase? How will I ever answer them all?"

In 1942, Jack was asked by his old tutor Wilson to contribute to the Oxford History of the English Language. Jack's specific assignment would be the 16th Century. Not to be only the highlights of giants like Spenser and Shakespeare but a complete survey of writers good and bad, it would be an immense undertaking. Before long Jack was referring to the ever-looming, ever time-consuming work as "Oh Hell!" the pronunciation of the acronym, O. H. E. L. Yet he knew "Oh Hell!" as the legacy of a scholar, would be as important as his *Allegory of Love*.

Jack also satisfied his desire for thoughtful scholarship that year by writing *Preface to Paradise Lost* for Oxford University Press. He dedicated it to Charles Williams. "Preface," however, was a gross understatement. The commentary lasted for eighteen chapters and filled 139 pages. Half of the "preface" defined what an epic was supposed to be. The other half described the Medieval Christianity that had shaped Milton's morality and recounted how Milton had differed from it.

Reviews in England and America were generally complimentary. After all, the *Preface* was a great help to those tackling Milton. Howbeit, some academics fumed over the work. How dared Jack lecture them on morality and Christianity? His evangelizing was permissable for common people, but it was presumptuous when it affected professors!

As if rising to the challenge, although the idea was not his, Jack became President of the Oxford University Socratic Club, an organization formed specifically to discuss religion. Stella Adwinkle of Somerville College, one of Oxford's five colleges for women, had approached him because the club was required to have a sponsor who was a don.

"Long overdue!" barked Jack to her request.

Later Warnie stated the obvious. "But isn't the membership of the club stacked against the atheists? Won't its opponents dismiss it as a not very cunningly disguised form of propaganda? What can be gained?"

"Intelligent people know argument has a life of its own," defended Jack. "We'll scour the *Who's Who* to find especially articulate champions of the atheists. I expect we'll not win every battle."

From then on during the term, the club met every Monday evening from eight-fifteen to ten-thirty. Usually about one hundred members attended. The typical format was a presentation, followed by rebuttal and discussion. In short order, Jack was expected to champion the Christian view every time. Students argued that in Jack's moderated radio talks, tutorials, and lectures he "talked in italics": every word was vital and penetrating. On the other hand, in his rebuttals at the Socratic Club, Jack spoke as he did with his closest friends on walks and at meetings of the Ink-lings: he was witty, boisterous, slashing, merciless, devastating. The Christian students loved it!

After a speaker for the opposition finished, the club's secretary would announce with breathless anticipation, "*Mr. C.S. Lewis* will now respond. . ."

On occasion, Dorothy Sayers, also known throughout the English-speaking world as one of the "Big Four" of the classic English mystery story, came to Oxford. One of Oxford's first women graduates, she was much like the Inklings: a superior intellect, about the same age as Lewis, and strong for Christianity. She liked Jack's apologetics, and Jack liked her own popular Christian works, *The Man Born to be King* and *Mind of the Maker*. He also truly admired her forceful personality, likening it to "a high wind." From Jack, the description was a great compliment because the intensity of storms thrilled him.

One evening Sayers assayed to advise Charles Williams on what he should do to become a successful best-selling author, but by the end of the evening, she was under his spell instead. "I must read *The Figure of Beatrice*. It's by Charles," she blazoned, beaming. Her life had taken a new direction: Dante and *The Divine Comedy*.

Sometimes people sought Jack out at the favorite public haunts of the Inklings. Once, at the Eagle and Child pub—known affectionately as the "Bird and Baby"—he was confronted by Roy Campbell, a fiery poet who was also a brawler. Although Jack had lampooned Campbell's poetry, Campbell had come not to fight but to enjoy the give-and-take. He had fought in the Spanish Civil War against the Communists. Both Tolkien and Jack despised Communism.

"But I also despise the Fascists you fought with," Jack stressed pointedly to Campbell. "I believe in democracy."

Only rarely did Jack's swashbuckling style carry over into his tutorials, but one particularly hardheaded, older student, who absolutely refused to read Matthew Arnold's

141

Sohrab and Rustum, provoked Jack into action. At his next tutorial, Jack quoted hundreds of lines from memory in his most rhythmic delivery.

"There," Jack finished, satisfied. "Now you must admit it has merit."

"It stinks," retorted the student.

"That's it then!" bellowed Jack. "The sword must settle it."

Amazingly Jack did have two swords in his sitting room, and the two actually clacked swords for a while as one of Jack's astonished friends looked on.

Nevertheless, such cavalier behavior with students was very unusual for Jack. In fact, his demeanor was intentionally low-key and unemotional. Very conscious that some pupils were only seventeen or eighteen, he usually extended quiet civility to his pupils, just as Smewgy had done for him. Scarcely ever did he bully them or even raise his voice.

As a rule, Jack met with each student for one hour a week. During the first meeting, he specified the background the pupil would need to master English Literature from Old English to 1821. "The great English writers assume a sound Biblical and classical background," he would advise a pupil. "Be certain to read the historical books of the Old Testament, Psalms, and the Gospels, particularly the book of Luke. If you read the Vulgate version, you can brush up on your Latin too." Though sorely tempted, Jack purposely never evangelized a pupil.

"But, Mr. Lewis, when do we read Shakespeare?"

"Oh, you will," he would assure, "but to understand Shakespeare best we must master the Bible and the classics. Don't bother with Greek. Read Virgil, Boethius, Ovid, and Cicero."

"Quite a load, sir," the student would sigh.

"Yes. To be sure," Jack would agree before continuing. "You also need to know how to scan hexameters." Inevitably, the pupil's face would pale. Analyzing the meter of classic poetry by quantity rather than stress numbed them with fear. "Now to the English writers," Jack would breeze, observing the student perk up. "Chaucer, Shakespeare, and Milton are imperative. Know them. At other various times, you're sure to encounter Malory, Spenser, Donne, Browne, Dryden, Pope, Swift, Johnson, and Wordsworth. Any questions?"

During the term, having studied and written an essay before each week's meeting, the pupil would take a chair in Jack's large sitting room and unwind during two or three minutes of polite conversation with him. Then the pupil would begin the lesson by reading his essay. Usually the essay was read in about fifteen minutes. Reading beyond half an hour was considered bad form; it left little time for discussion.

Jack had several favorite comments at the conclusion of the reading. "There may be something in what you say" meant the essay was bad. "There is something in what you say" indicated the essay was barely acceptable, as did "Too much straw and not enough bricks." If the essay was good, he would allow, "There is a good deal in what you say." "Much of that was very well said" recognized an outstanding essay.

Next, Jack, who had taken notes, would direct, "Now we shall discuss these points in your essay: verbal structure, rhythm, and clarity. Also, to remind you that I'm no great fan of clichés and figures of speech, we shall discuss precision."

The main points of communicating having been discussed, Jack and his pupil would finally examine the material under study. Occasionally Jack would astonish his pupil by quoting verse after verse of *Paradise Lost*. Even more amazing was his gift of instant entry into the classic. If a pupil would quote one line, Jack would instantly quote subsequent lines. His memory was photographic.

Though remaining frank in his opinions, through the years his Christianity compelled him more and more to soften criticism with a joke or praise. "That's really quite imaginative. Perhaps we can discuss some mistakes to improve your future work. . ."

At the end of each term, Jack reserved a private room at Magdalen and gave a dinner party for his pupils. For this event, he entertained in the raucous way he did with his closest friends, in the way his father had done with his friends. To Jack, the celebration was almost a rite of passage for the pupil, so he conducted it like a Medieval rite, bringing forth not bawdy songs, but what he called "bawdry" songs, clever songs of coarse humor and irreverence.

"In the Middle Ages," he reminded his pupils, "this type of a festive gathering of men brought forth devotions and tragedies as well as bawdry songs—all in an oral tradition, of course—authors now long unknown."

Meanwhile, Jack's works outside of Oxford continued to flourish. In July of 1942, Geoffrey Bles published Jack's two series of radio talks, "Right and Wrong" and "What Christians Believe," as *Broadcast Talks*. Jack was so well known now that no other title was necessary. A new, third series of talks, called "Christian Behavior," encouraged Christians to pursue holy lives, and was scheduled to be published as *Christian Behavior* in 1943.

Broadcast Talks presented to the layman in the most comprehensible English Jack's arguments for that basic Christianity recognized by Protestants and Catholics alike. There is an underlying law of morality, he insisted, that all mankind intuitively knows is the right way to behave. This suggests a "mind" rules the universe. Yet, mankind constantly misbehaves anyway. Therein lies a great paradox: if the "mind" is not good, mankind is lost; if the "mind" is good, mankind is in dire trouble for misbehaving!

In his treatise, Jack then reviewed the great religions. He propounded that only those religions that believe in a creator outside the universe deal with the problem of a loving God permitting evil and suffering: Judaism, Islam, and Christianity. And why do Christians believe Christ is also God? Because Christ is an historical fact; because He claimed to be God; because He died and is alive again—hundreds of witnesses saw Him both before and after the resurrection.

Initial belief is but one step. The next step is to live as a Christian. All mankind recognizes the goodness of the four cardinal virtues: prudence or common sense; temperance or self-control; justice or fairness; and fortitude or courage. The Christian has three more virtues: hope, that continual looking forward to God's eternal world; faith, to ward off the black moments of disbelief or suffering; and charity, the greatest virtue of all, loving as God loves.

A Christian who tries to treat everyone kindly finds himself liking more and more people, even people he could not have imagined himself liking initially, but Christian charity must be practiced even when the Christian doesn't "feel" loving. When the Christian "feels" no real love of God, he acts as one acts who does love God. Jack insisted that when this is done, love will come. Thus he concluded *Broadcast Talks*.

In 1943 Jack received from J.B. Phillips the clergyman's own translation of Paul's letter to the Colossians. Phillips was proposing no less than translating all the letters of Paul into modern English! Jack read a passage that had always troubled him, even though he was a superb translator of Greek himself.

"I see the meaning clearly now," he blurted. "It's like seeing a familiar picture after its been cleaned."

Jack was genuinely pleased with Phillips' translation of Colossians. He wrote him:

> *I hope very much you will carry out your*
> *plan of doing all the epistles. Of course*
> *you'll be opposed tooth and nail by all the*
> *"cultured". . .who say you're only spoiling*
> *"the beauty" of (the King James version). . .[1]*

Jack did not object to a qualified scholar translating the Greek of the New Testament into the common language of the modern Englishman. Oh yes, he loved the poetry of the King James version, but hadn't it become a luxury of the scholarly? How many modern Englishmen knew the subtleties of 17th-century English? And hadn't Jack advanced his apologetics the same way, moving away from troublesome jargon to the simplest modern language possible?

The success of *The Screwtape Letters* still reverberated. By 1943 the American press had picked up on it. The *New York Times* commented:

> *"The devil," said Thomas More, "cannot*
> *endure being mocked," and which, if correct,*
> *means that somewhere in the inferno there*
> *must be considerable annoyance. . .*

The *Saturday Review of Literature* was even more impressed:

> *Whatever you may think of the theses of Mr.*
> *Lewis, presented as they are in a bizarre and*
> *slandicular manner, the fact remains that there*

146

is a spectacular and satisfactory nova in the bleak sky of satire. . .

The Screwtape Letters not only sold well itself in America but created demand for Jack's previous works: *The Problem of Pain*, *Out of the Silent Planet*, and *Broadcast Talks* (printed in America as *Case for Christianity*.) Even *Pilgrim's Regress* was reprinted and sold well in America, because all of these reissued books received good reviews in American magazines and newspapers.

Of *Case for Christianity*, the magazine *Christian Century* commented:

> *Two series of radio talks. . .converge to the same conclusion by different approaches. The first argues from the general sense of right and wrong to the existence of a moral law which is more than social habit or the rationalization of self-interest. The second shows the impossibility of atheism as an explanation of the world and man. . .The author is at particular pains to avoid theological lingo and to stress the note of plain common sense. . .*

The magazine *Catholic World* liked *Case for Christianity* too:

> *. . .it says very many things that desperately need to be said. Armies of men are groping their way back to the religion of Christ; this book will facilitate greatly that sacred journey. . .*

The Problem of Pain received a glowing review from the *Weekly Book Review*:

> *Mr. Lewis, author of* The Screwtape Letters, *is no doubt the ablest contemporary. . .(for) the exposition of the Christian position. . .The average man will. . .(be) able to come to grips with distressing facts. . .It not only makes uncommon good sense, but it is great writing. Perhaps Mr. Lewis succeeds better with straight argument than he does with parable. . .*

Because of its sheer entertainment value, American reviews of *Out of the Silent Planet* abounded. The *New York Times* reported:

> *The author's Miltonic love of light gives his descriptions of space real splendor. His narrative flows easily. . .it has its compelling moments when the reader loses himself in the make-believe, identifies himself with the hero. . .*

The *Saturday Review of Literature* stated:

> *(Out of the Silent Planet). . .is delightful; and its author, Fellow and Tutor of Magdalen, a most distinguished writer. . .*

The *New Yorker* reviewed *Out of the Silent Planet* very briefly, but made the point:

> *. . .A journey-to-Mars fantasy that is almost as good as the early H.G. Wells. The writing is*

miles above the usual (science fiction) level. . .

Publishers were now slavering after the sequel to *Out of the Silent Planet*. Jack knew exactly what he wanted to write—he just had to find the time in which to do it. His second space fiction would again involve the "good" man Ransom and the "evil" scientist Weston, but this time on Venus, or "Perelandra," as he called it. The time of the story would be before the Fall, and the vast watery world of Perelandra would be in complete harmony. There would be an Adam and an Eve, under different names, of course. Weston would represent the devil, trying to tempt "Eve" to disobey.

Jack had no deluded image of Adam and Eve as primitive, hairy simpletons. No, his image, already expressed in *The Problem of Pain* and his *Preface to Paradise Lost*, was quite the opposite. All great thinkers since Saint Augustine deemed humans before the Fall to be vastly superior to humans who followed—they were supremely in tune with nature, themselves, and God. They exercised their will over all the animals. They could will their bodies to do anything. They talked to God face to face.

"If such a man or woman were to appear among us," averred Jack, "the holiest one among us would immediately be on his knees."

The astonishing rate at which Jack was publishing would never have been possible under a normal workload at Oxford, but most of the students were still off fighting a war. Having never been busier, he wondered how he would cope with the workload after the war. Because of the staggering volume of letters, they worked out a routine by which Warnie could help Jack answer each one. Jack would read a letter and jot a thoughtful answer on it. Warnie, who had taught himself to type while organizing the Lewis papers, would then type the response for Jack's signature. Eventually, Warnie knew exactly how Jack would answer the more routine letters, and he began to answer them for Jack. Jack had only to sign at the bottom. Because Jack's response would not have been different, neither brother considered the method dishonest at all. Through this cooperation, Jack began noticing that Warnie was indeed a very gifted writer.

Warnie spent much more time at the Kilns now than Jack, who seemed committed at every moment. Jack's socializing at the Kilns had almost stopped. His get-togethers with the Inklings and the Socratic Club—even his frequent pub visits to the "Bird and Baby"—seemed a natural extension of his life's work rather than socializing. The Kilns grew more and more remote. Jack knew failing health was making Mrs. Moore, now 70, very cantankerous, but Warnie, irritated by her, hinted that she was becoming irrational. For years already, Warnie had silently but obviously sympathized with Maureen in squabbles with her mother. Besides that, Mrs. Moore's generosity and kindness presumed on those in the household. She was not the one who walked Troodles and Mr. Papworth and Bruce and all the other dogs she took in. Nor was the busy Paxford. No, the dogs were cared for by Jack and Warnie. And now that Jack was rarely present, their keeper was barely-willing Warnie. "I calculate I've wasted several months of my life just walking dogs," Warnie groused to Jack one evening.

In 1943 Oxford University Press published Jack's *Abolition of Man*. The book, though based on a series of lectures, was aimed at the general public, and it missed the mark. It had none of the warmth and strength of his other works. It was too detached, too scholarly. Jack was convinced it was a very important work: it did no less than point out how and why our modern society was going haywire. Maniacs like Hitler and Stalin, however, should have made the point obvious.

The book also failed to reach the intellectuals. The new philosophers at Oxford, adherents of "logical positivism," a new approach which was tearing down all absolute morality, nit-picked every definition that defended absolutes. Could it be proved mathematically? If not, it was meaningless. So beauty and ugliness were only relative at best, and right and wrong meant nothing at all.

"I regret more than anything that Abolition of Man failed as a popular book," sorrowed Jack.

"Some might say it's not so enjoyable to read," evaded Warnie tactfully.

"Deadly bore, is it?"

Jack would have to make the point of *Abolition of Man* in another way. Already his mind was cranking. The dread destroyers of order and decency would be the villains of his next space fiction, the conclusion of his trilogy. But that book would have to wait its turn. . .

twelve

Mixed Reviews

*I*n 1943, the second book of Jack's space trilogy was published. *Perelandra* was a smashing success with most reviewers, English and American, religious and secular. America's *Catholic World* wrote:

> *Readers who enjoy these interplanetary specu-*
> *lations will find this experiment 'on the side of*
> *the angels.'*

The *Christian Science Monitor* added:

> *"Mr. Lewis' imagination is luxurious and schol-*
> *arly, and his power of suspense considerable."*

The *New York Times* raved about *Perelandra*:

> *One of the most exciting stories since H.G.*
> *Wells' "Invisible Man," Mr. Lewis. . .has an*
> *equal genius for making his fantasies livable.*
> *Since Perelandra is apparently a planet much*
> *resembling Paradise, he has here accomplished*
> *a peculiarly difficult job—that of representing*
> *the sights, sounds, smells and all the unfamiliar*
> *physical sensations of a state of perfection. . .*

In England, Jack's TLS review was glowing, calling the

book:

> . . .*(a) remarkable study. . .(showing) a rare*
> *power of inventive imagination, and something*
> *of the graphic vigor of language. . .*

Commonweal praised the book saying:
> *from all standpoints, far superior to other tales*
> *of interplanetary adventures.*

Personally Jack felt it was his best fiction yet, but resentment was stirring among those who embraced the glory of science and humanism, and even atheism, because Jack was becoming too successful. Some reviews were sprinkled with such unfavorable comments as, "For the reviewer, *Perelandra* . . .was a place of nightmare horror," "Mr. Lewis loads the dice heavily," "metaphysical abracadabra," and "nonsense."

Also in 1943, Geoffrey Bles published *Christian Behavior*, the next installment of Jack's radio broadcasts. No longer were his religious books reviewed only by *Catholic World, Christian Century,* and other religious periodicals, although these certainly praised *Christian Behavior*. Now his religious exposition was noted by the secular press, especially in America. The *New York Times* praised the book and said of Jack:

> . . .*His mind is very clear; his style exhibits*
> *the costly simplicity that is achieved only after*
> *much learning and thinking and pruning*
> *away of non-essentials. . .*

In 1944 Geoffrey Bles published *Beyond Personality: The Christian Idea of God*, a compilation of more of Jack's radio talks, and his most ambitious effort at theology yet. Many advised him not to do it because he explored the very nature of God; he asserted man is alive and part of the "bios" but not part of "zoe," or the spiritual life that exists in God; he advocated that the whole purpose of our existence is to be taken into the life of God.

Jack further explained the Christian concept of the Trinity: three Gods in One. God is the spiritual being we are trying to reach and reflect. Christ is the only real source of our knowledge of God. The Holy Spirit is the part of God within us. Because God is not in Time, He can attend personally to each individual. When we become Christ-like, we are drawn into God.

Beyond Personality was also evaluated by an array of reviewers. The *New York Times* finally stated what was common knowledge now:

> . . .*Mr. Lewis, the layman of Oxford, continues to be the major apostle of Christian faith for the man in the street wherever he may be strolling along the sidewalk. In his latest installment of what is becoming a comprehensive survey of truths. . .The pages are crowded as ever with apt illustration, humorous ways of putting things, and searching rejoinders to negative plausibilities. . .*

The *Weekly Book Review* added its praise:
> *No wonder he is popular. . .His clarity of thought and simplicity of expression have a magic about them which makes plain the most abstruse problems of theological speculation. . .*

Religious publications were ecstatic with his success. *Catholic World* acclaimed, "gifted Mr. Lewis. . .(has an) almost unique ability to make abstractions intelligible and interesting." *Churchman* applauded: "once again this brilliant author. . .endeavors to explain the orthodox Christian faith in the simplest terms."

Jack now devoted much of his time to writing two books scheduled for publication in 1945, his third space fiction and another fiction unlike any he had done: *The Great Divorce*. ("Divorce" referred to the chasm between heaven and hell.) Jack's book would be a loose rewrite of Dante's trip in *The Divine Comedy* through modern eyes. For instance, Jack's guide, instead of Virgil, is his own mentor, George MacDonald, and a busload of egotistical sinners are shown heaven, where they struggle with all their might to preserve their damnable identities.

After *The Great Divorce* was published, it was praised by the *New York Times*, the *New Yorker*, the *Library Journal*, and the *Weekly Book Review*. Other reviews were lukewarm, like the review in TLS. A few, like the one in *Kirkus*, expressed disappointment. A very few, like the one in the *Spectator*, were antagonistic. As TLS pointed out: "Those who find themselves in agreement with the arguments put up by the Ghosts for not being saved will be unlikely to finish this book!"

All the Inklings but Tolkien seemed to approve Jack's clever device for fiction in *The Great Divorce*. Tolkien assessed, "Dante is spiteful and malicious. He's all about petty people in petty situations." Thus he condemned one of Jack's heroes and indirectly Jack's fiction too.

Jack's third space fiction, *That Hideous Strength*, particularly caused a rift between himself and Tolkien. Tolkien was writing a book all the Inklings called *The New Hobbit*, regardless that its official title was to be *The Lord of the Rings*. Tolkien's style had changed in this new work. The narrative was faster paced and more compelling. The message of the myth was enormous. Jack, convinced that *The Lord of the Rings* could potentially be a major work of the century if Tolkien could sustain it, encouraged Tolkien more than anyone else. Curiously, however, Tolkien had to be prodded and prodded. Sometimes he would put down *The New Hobbit* and not work on it for months and months. Jack was the catalyst that kept the effort going.

Yet when Jack read to the Inklings his third space fiction, *That Hideous Strength*, Tolkien openly despised it. "Too many themes are jumbled together," he carped. Moreover, Tolkien thought Jack was pandering to Charles Williams by introducing King Arthur themes, and he made no effort to conceal his opinion.

The first two fictions, especially *Perelandra*, were pared to the bone, lean and magnificent. In this book, Jack had been very much inspired by Williams. He had indulged his imagination; he had indulged friends. In this book, he had alluded to both Tolkien and Barfield; he had created one character who was clearly his old tutor Kirkpatrick; and he had metamorphosed Ransom into an image of Charles Williams!

"Tolkien considers *That Hideous Strength* to be a fat, sloppy, indulgent mess," Jack repined to Warnie. "Other than that he likes it," he quipped facetiously.

Many reviewers agreed the book was disappointing and criticized Jack for weaknesses that were usually his strengths. *Catholic World* suggested "drastic pruning" could have made it "timely and rousing." *Churchman* found the characters and motives "sometimes incomprehensible." The Saturday Review of Literature complained "the redemption of one intellectual opportunist" seemed poor reward for reading such a tome.

So the reviews confirmed that truth had been in Tolkien's carping, but his jealousy over Charles Williams was difficult to ignore. That Jack enjoyed the company of Williams more than anyone he had met—other than Owen Barfield—was true. Jack still reckoned Barfield the greatest intellect he had ever known, but Charles Williams was a close second. Despite Tolkien's jealousy, Jack promoted Williams all the more. Jack hoped that, with his backing, Charles Williams could acquire a post at Oxford as Professor of Poetry, his lack of a college degree notwithstanding. Preliminarily, Jack helped Williams revise what many thought was his best supernatural thriller, *All Hallows' Eve*. Jack also used his influence with Geoffrey Bles to procure Williams a contract for a book on forgiveness in their Christian Challenge Series.

Mere days after World War II ended in May of 1945, Jack received his greatest blow since his father had died in 1929. Charles Williams, only fifty-eight, died in what Jack had presumed was minor surgery. Stunned by Williams' death, Jack attempted to sort out his feelings in verse:

> *Your death blows a strange bugle call,*
> *friend, and all is hard*
> *To see plainly or record truly.*
> *The new light imposes change,*
> *Re-adjusts all a life-landscape*
> *as it thrusts down its probe from the sky,*
> *To create shadows, to reveal waters,*
> *to erect hills and deepen glens.*
> *The slant alters. I can't see the old contours.*
> *T's a larger world*
> *Than I once thought it. I wince, caught in*
> *the bleak air that blows on the ridge.*
> *Is it the sting of the great winter,*
> *the world waning? Or the cold of spring?*

> *A hard question and worth talking a whole*
> *night on.*
> *But with whom?*
> *Of whom now can I ask guidance?*
> *With what friend concerning your death*
> *Is it worth while to exchange thoughts*
> *unless—oh, unless it were you?[1]*

Jack sensed his presence, as if Williams were in a state of bliss yet somehow able to look upon the living. Jack felt pain and loss, but no resentment—Christ had changed that. How could a Christian resent a friend going on to paradise?

Because Jack felt a great debt to Williams for expanding his imagination, he had solicited essays from friends that were to be a farewell gift to Williams as he left for London. Now the essays by Jack, Tolkien, Dorothy Sayers, Owen Barfield, and other contributors would be a memorial. Jack could not bring himself to change the title: *Essays Presented to Charles Williams.*

In the book he depicted Williams, the man:

> *In appearance he was tall, slim, and straight*
> *as a boy, though gray-haired. His face we*
> *thought ugly. . .but the moment he spoke it*
> *became. . .like the face of an angel. . .No*
> *man whom I have known was at the same*
> *time less affected and more flamboyant in*
> *his manners: and also more playful. . .[2]*

Jack had certainly been victimized by his playfulness. Once Williams had engineered a lunch meeting between Jack and his long-time nemesis, T.S. Eliot. As the two enemies carried on an interminable icy conversation, Williams enjoyed the occasion enormously. Jack had harbored no grudge. Perhaps the meeting might have been a success. Was it Williams' fault? Or the fault of two proud antagonists?

> *That face. . .comes back to me. . .distorted*
> *into helpless laughter at some innocently*
> *broad buffoonery or eagerly stretched for-*
> *ward in the cut and parry of prolonged,*
> *fierce. . .argument. . .The talk might turn in*
> *almost any direction,. . .but wherever it went,*
> *Williams was ready for it. . .on the rare occa-*
> *sions when he did not turn up. . .liveliness*
> *and cohesion had been withdrawn from the*
> *whole party; lacking him, we did not com-*
> *pletely possess one another. . .*[3]

The essays themselves were not tribute enough for Jack. In a tribute he entitled *Arthurian Torso,* he gathered several unpublished chapters that Williams had written on the King Arthur legends, then added his own unstinting praise on Williams' poetry called the Taliessin cycle. Jack asserted that in certain of these poems Williams had produced word music unsurpassed by any other poet of the Twentieth Century. Both tributes were eventually published by Williams' own publisher, Oxford University Press.

"These tributes to Williams have jogged me into also acknowledging my debt to George MacDonald," Jack told Warnie.

"Your old master since the age of seventeen!" Warnie yelped.

"The same," declared Jack. "MacDonald captivated me because I was naturally drawn toward 'otherness,' but thanks to MacDonald I was lured by holiness instead of the occult."

Jack compiled an anthology of excerpts from MacDonald's writings that illuminated Christianity, then wrote a preface of about 4000 words. Not fawning and uncritical, he acknowledged that MacDonald was not a writer of the first rank, but that he had so successfully created myth that it overcame writing too often florid and verbose. Without reservation Jack could recommend his fantasies: *Phantastes*, *Lilith*, and the two "Curdie" books. Jack knew others, such as J.R.R. Tolkien, W.H. Auden, and G.K. Chesterton, shared his high opinion of MacDonald's myth-making. The anthology was published in 1946.

Jack continued to explain the truths of Christianity, addressing any stumbling block that caused people to turn away from finding Christ. What was mentioned as a stumbling block more often than the miracles in the Bible? How often had Jack heard people mutter, "If only it weren't for the miracles. . ."?

Thus, in his book *Miracles*, virtually completed in 1945 but not published until 1947, Jack's goal was no less than to convince skeptics the miracles were not unusual at all—for God. It was a very bold book, finished only through inspiration gained from Charles Williams. In it, Jack argued powerfully that not supernaturalism but naturalism was self-contradictory. His book was no less than a proof of the supernatural.

Religious publications like *Christian Century* openly praised *Miracles*, but reviews in secular publications were cautious. Praising the book seemed too much like substantiating supernaturalism. Most reviewers, therefore, recommended the book, yet tried not to endorse the ideas. TLS said:

> *Mr. Lewis casts his net fairly wide. . .some*
> *points are overlooked which would have*

found a place in a more analytical account. . .
it would seem that Mr. Lewis' book lacks a
final element of persuasiveness. . .In spite of
these reserves, Mr. Lewis has produced an
impressive book. . .

Miracles cemented with the public his reputation as a popular apologist for Christianity. He was featured on the cover of the American magazine, *Time*. Inside, a lengthy article teemed with inaccuracies and rumors about his private life. The reporter had assumed that any questions unable to be answered by Jack's friends indicated Jack was secretive. The magazine raised the possibility that Jack was a hypocrite who simply wrote for money. Jack did not bother to refute the charge by revealing that profits from his religious books went to charity.

Nevertheless, Jack, the literary critic, was pleased with some of the writing in *Time*. The article acknowledged his debt to George MacDonald and Charles Williams. And descriptions of himself were amusing:

The lecturer (Jack), a. . .thickset man with a
ruddy face and a big voice, was coming to the
end of his talk. Gathering up his notes and
books, he tucked his horn-rimmed spectacles
into the pocket of his tweed jacket and picked
up his mortarboard. Still talking—to the
accompaniment of occasional appreciative
laughs and squeals—he leaned over to return
the watch he had borrowed from a student in
the front row. As he ended his final sentence,
he stepped off the platform. The maneuver
gained him a head start on the rush of students

down the center aisle. Once in the street, he
strode rapidly—his black gown billowing
behind his gray flannel trousers. . .

True enough. The article was also faithful to mention his extraordinary teaching load during the post-war years. It included some nice quotes on the absurdities of pantheism and the wish for sexual pleasure in heaven. The reporter confirmed Jack's belief that many of the faculty were jealous of his success, some to the point of promoting the lie that he wrote to make lots of money. Some complained instead about his bluntness. It was true; he was blunt.

The article, no matter how lengthy, failed to cover even a tenth of Jack's responsibilities. In spite of Jack's deliberate effort to keep his pupils at a distance emotionally, some came to him with problems. One student came to him in desperation. "I loaned a large sum of money to someone and he won't repay me. Now I'm short."

"Never loan large sums of money," advised Jack. "Give a small amount of money."

"I see. . ." moaned the student in dejection.

"I belong to a group of people who help deserving cases like yours. I'll put your case before them," Jack offered. In fact, Jack was the one who gave the student the money he needed.

Another time Jack was confronted by an even more desperate undergraduate. The student, who suffered a chronic stutter, had experienced a succession of setbacks: severe bronchitis, rejection from a woman, malaise, and finally severe depression. He requested his examinations to be delayed, even hinting at suicide.

"Didn't you say your home was nearly destroyed by a bomb during the war?" probed Jack.

"Y. . .y. . .yes."

"And yet you were spared, while hundreds of thousands of your countrymen were not. How can you be so ungrateful?" But Jack's voice was gentle, not reproachful. The student recovered.

The *Time* article quoted the Oxford undergraduate magazine, *Cherwell*, in which Jack had warned:

> *Christianity is now "on the map" among the younger (students). . .the days of simple "unfaith" are as dead as those of "simple faith". . .(yet) we must remember that widespread and lively interest in the subject is precisely what we call a fashion. . . Whatever in our present success mere fashion has given us, mere fashion will presently withdraw. The real conversions will remain, but nothing else will. . . we must cherish no picture of the present intellectual movement simply growing and spreading and finally reclaiming millions by sweet reasonableness. . .*

Jack knew all too well that to many Christianity was initially appealing and finally, as they learned more of it, repulsive. Christianity was hard. It demanded total surrender and exposed the great gulf between Nature and the Supernatural.

"Even the Socratic Club is full of fair-weather student followers," he lamented to Warnie. "We must never be complacent."

On February 2, 1948, when the secretary of the Socratic Club announced, "Our topic today is 'Miracles: A Reply to Mr. C.S. Lewis,'" one of the new philosophers, Elizabeth Anscombe, rose and attempted to destroy his argument. Jack found himself as usual, refuting the opposition. He was aggressive, bullying in his defense. And the evening became one of his worst memories!

thirteen

Changes

E lizabeth Anscombe was no shrinking violet. Large and beefy like Jack, she wore pants and even smoked cigars! Worse than that, though, she was brilliant enough to hopelessly entangle Jack in definitions. As a logical positivist, she could never be persuaded with mathematics. She also made him appear to be waffling. Later, although his loyal followers insisted he had won the debate, he was very depressed.

"Lord, how will one ever communicate right and wrong, much less the glory of Christ, with the modern philosophers and their unfortunate disciples?" pleaded Jack.

Some started a rumor that Jack was so depressed by Anscombe's thrashing that he refused to write any further apologetics. This was utter nonsense because Jack had told the *Time* reporter six months before the confrontation with Anscombe that he was planning no more apologetics in the near future. For the present, he had written what he wanted to write and was moving back into fiction in some form.

"I won't refute every malicious rumor," determined Jack. "Surely intelligent people can decipher the truth." And he prayed that they would. Christ was now his anchor.

Jack was pleased to see J.B. Phillips' translation of the letters of Paul finally in print. He had certainly done his part in nudging it to fruition. After many rejections, his own publisher, Geoffrey Bles, had agreed to publish it on his recommendation. Jack had suggested the title, *Letters to Young*

Churches, and written the preface, pointing out that the 1600's traditionalists had also objected to the new version being authorized by King James! He made another point too: the King James version is *not* a translation of the New Testament in its original Greek; the King James version is a translation of a Latin translation of the original Greek. "As beautiful as the King James version is, who could object to a more direct approach by a modern scholar?" Jack queried.

Possibly on the basis of Jack's appeal and the prominent display of his name on the dust jacket, *Letters to Young Churches* sold very well right from the beginning and by its own merit soon gained a life of its own. It steadily gained popularity until it appeared it would actually become a bestseller.

Despite the popular press lauding Jack as the great champion for Christianity, life seemed sour to him in 1948. He turned fifty. The teaching load was enormous. He couldn't change the fact that Williams was dead. Tolkien was peevish and disagreeable. And the Oxford he saw every day was more and more hostile. In their cultured opinion, wearing Christianity on one's sleeve, like he was doing, was rather unfashionable. Day-to-day life at Magdalen was more and more stressful, and the sad truth was that the Kilns offered no relief. In fact, Jack went there with a sense of dread. Rationing of food had everyone on edge. Now even potatoes, which they relied on as their main "filler," were rationed. What quarrel would greet Jack at the Kilns? With whom was Mrs. Moore fighting now? The cook? A new maid perhaps?

Was Warnie of help? Yes, when he was not drinking heavily. Once or twice a year now, he binged, usually disappearing to visit friends who also drank or Ireland to drink anywhere. Jack expected a call for him to come to Warnie's aid at any time. During Warnie's binges, his drinking accelerated until he was in a deathlike stupor. Then Jack would find some hospital or rest home to take him in until he recovered. Yet, even in this turmoil, the hope offered by Christ sustained Jack, and his work continued.

"All my fiction progresses in images," he freely revealed, "like I am watching a movie."

Many years before—perhaps when he had been only sixteen—he had seen a vision of a faun carrying an umbrella and a parcel through a snowy wood. As the war began and the schoolgirls from London arrived in 1939, he actually transcribed some of the story about the faun, his main characters none other than four children who had left London because of the war: Ann, Martin, Rose, and Peter. They stayed with a very old professor.

Six years later, in 1945, Jack perused the manuscript of a children's story by Roger Green, a former pupil. Some of its elements remained vividly with Jack. In 1948 he resumed his own story, and, with Green's permission—Green had never published his narrative—Jack incorporated some of Green's ideas. The children became Susan, Lucy, Edmund, and Peter Pevensie. Soon Jack had created the fantasy world of Narnia, which the children visited by walking through a magic wardrobe in the professor's house. Jack had been dreaming about lions, and the story crystallized when he introduced Christ in the form of a magnificent lion named Aslan. By Christmas of 1948 the story was finished. By early 1949 he rehearsed it to Tolkien.

"Tolkien despises it," he reported to Warnie later. "He says I have a worthless jumble of different mythologies."

Jack's publisher, Geoffrey Bles, was not enthusiastic about the story either. Now dubbed *The Lion, the Witch, and the Wardrobe*, it combined Christianity, Santa Claus, talking animals, fauns, witches, and real people. On the other hand, Jack did have a name that sold books, so Bles would risk the project. Perhaps, Bles suggested, Jack could write a subsequent episode; a series might allow them to recover their investment. So Jack forged ahead with the sequel, *Prince Caspian*. For the first time in a long time, Geoffrey Bles would not go ahead straightaway with one of Jack's books.

"Can you believe it! He even hinted he might want to see a third book in the series before he proceeds," he fumed to Mrs. Moore.

Life at Oxford seemed diminished for Jack too. He no longer enjoyed the Socratic Club, though serving as president since its inception. He was tired of fending off the logical positivism of atheists and agnostics.

Besides his discontent with the Socratic Club, Jack was disgusted about being denied a professorship, even after many years. Tolkien had been a full professor since 1945. (Once again, although Jack gave Tolkien his full support whether in the area of writing or academic pursuits—like the curriculum, Tolkien offered Jack only the most tepid support in return.) Essentially, Jack was exhausted. Full professors did not have to tutor, but he, without the professorship, was still tutoring after twenty-five years!

The years immediately after the war had been particularly difficult. Many soldiers had returned to resume their studies. Tutoring had never been a greater burden, requiring morning, afternoon, and evening sessions, but Jack, never one to slight his duties, had simply refused to cheat a pupil out of what was rightly his.

Demands on Jack's energies intensified as Warnie's drinking reached new levels. He was at Malvern bingeing again. Already completely exhausted, Jack became depressed. Nonetheless, he persistently strove to finish his enormous volume of "Oh Hell!"—the Oxford History of English

Literature. One night in June of 1949 at the Kilns, Jack began to hallucinate. Thankfully, Mrs. Moore, not healthy herself, had the presence of mind to call the ambulance. Thus, when Warnie returned, Jack was in the hospital receiving shot after shot of penicillin.

"Humphrey says I was run down," Jack murmured to Warnie. "The first germ that came along knocked me over." (His doctor, Robert Havard, who had attended Inkling meetings, was called "Humphrey.")

"You'll be back on your feet in a few days. Look at me. I'm over my insomnia," Warnie chirped.

But Warnie disappeared to binge again. This time he went to Ireland. He insisted he would not drink, or, if he did, he would control it. That delusion worried Jack. Days later he had to rush to Ireland; Warnie was virtually being detained in an asylum because he was so uncontrollable. Jack realized he could no longer hide Warnie's drinking. No longer would he speak of Warnie suffering from "insomnia" or "nerves." Warnie was an alcoholic. Humbly, Jack sought the advice of his closest friends.

"Is it a moral dilemma?" he besought Tolkien. "Warnie is the meekest of men. Or is it medical? Or both? Should I 'show my teeth' to discourage him from more bouts?"

For once, Jack even sought advice outside his usual close circle. "Only the alcoholic stops drinking," counseled those wise in the ways of drinkers. Jack was disheartened, aware that Warnie still deluded himself about drinking, purporting that he could still drink, he just needed to exert more will power. Deep inside, Jack knew only one hope for Warnie. So he prayed.

Life at Oxford continued to ebb. The evening of October 27, 1949, was numbing. "No one showed up for the Inkling meeting," brooded Warnie, sober again.

The Inklings never met again. The end had been coming. Jack had not read any of his work to the group since Tolkien had savaged *The Lion, the Witch, and the Wardrobe.* As well, because Hugo Dyson had repeatedly ridiculed *The Lord of the Rings*, Tolkien had not presented any of his work since 1947!

Meanwhile, Warnie, in his sober moments, labored as Jack's secretary. "Well, here's another feminine admirer from America," he teased Jack in 1950, waving a letter.

Jack reached for it somewhat reluctantly. "Not another celebrity worshipper, I hope." Moments later, however, he was chuckling. "She writes very well. Just the kind of humor I like too. What's her name? Joy Gresham. . ." He sat down and immediately composed the brilliant reply it demanded.

Over the next months, Jack exchanged letters with Joy Gresham. Having steady correspondents who considered him their spiritual mentor because of his books was not at all unusual for Jack. He had several such "pen-friends." Joy was a writer with two small boys and a husband who resented her writing. In no way did she express any self pity, but Jack, because of his own difficulties, could tell her life was not smooth. As Joy continually posed conundrums that corroded her newly acquired Christianity, Jack felt obligated to destroy them one by one.

In April, 1950, Mrs. Moore, now seventy-seven, frightened Jack. She was obviously senile and kept falling out of bed. To ensure that she was properly cared for, Jack took her to Rest-holme. Now beyond reach mentally, when she wasn't cursing the nursing home, she was inventing tragic news.

"Very bad news about Maureen," she whined to Warnie when he visited her. "Killed."

Although life at the Kilns was less stressful now—when Warnie was not drinking—the rest of Jack's life still seemed sour. A few friends met very informally every

Tuesday night at the 'Bird and Baby,' but the assemblage was no substitute for the Inklings. The very atmosphere at Oxford felt hostile. Tolkien's peevishness intensified because he was unable to find a publisher for *The Lord of the Rings*. The apparent ease with which Jack wrote and was published seemed to irritate him.

Jack wished for his previous lack of trouble in getting published. Geoffrey Bles refused to publish *The Lion, the Witch, and the Wardrobe* until he had in hand Jack's third book, *The Voyage of the Dawn Treader*. When the first book was finally published in the fall of 1950, it received favorable but cautious reviews. Reviewers admitted Jack's writing was superb as usual, but asserted that modern children, who want to know how to cope with real-life problems, dislike moralistic fairy stories. Critics deemed Jack's characters too old-fashioned, too simple, too straight forward, and, some, altogether too scary! All in all the book was not thought likely to appeal to modern children.

"We'll wait and see how it sells for Christmas," drawled the publisher, trying to remain optimistic. "Then we'll publish one a year just before Christmas," he strategized with little conviction.

By late 1950, Jack admitted to himself that Mrs. Moore had put him under great stress for several years. Without her presence, the Kilns was now a peaceful home. Nonetheless, he faithfully prayed for her and asked friends to pray for her too. He also visited her nearly every afternoon. Sometimes she raved angrily; sometimes she babbled like a child. He assured himself she would not have been one bit happier at the Kilns. Gradually, his health improved as he enjoyed more walks and even began swimming again at Parson's Pleasure.

In January of 1951, Mrs. Moore died from influenza at the age of seventy-eight and was buried in the churchyard of Holy

Trinity Church in nearby Headington Quarry. Jack suffered greatly; he was very attached to her. Guilt of his own pettiness and stinginess haunted him too, because he had begun to resent the crushing expense of Restholme. Little by little, he realized that he worried about finances just like his father had. He also noticed something else. He preferred a rigid church service just like his father had. Jack understood now that the predictability of form, unlike the distraction of something novel, allowed him to focus more intensely on prayer.

Although Warnie had been too drunk to attend Mrs. Moore's funeral, Jack knew from experience he was not beginning one of his customary binges. Eagerly he rushed off to Ireland to visit Arthur. After only a few days, he felt happier than he had in many years, much prayer having helped him accept that feeling without guilt. Then sales of *The Lion, the Witch, and the Wardrobe* skyrocketed. The Narnia story seemed to be exactly what the children wanted.

By the time Jack's second Narnia book was published before Christmas in 1951 and was selling as well as the first, Tolkien was still searching for a publisher for *The Lord of the Rings*. Meanwhile Jack slightly revised *Broadcast Talks*, *Christian Behavior*, and *Beyond Personality* and combined them into one book: *Mere Christianity*. It was an immediate bestseller in 1952.

When Jack's third Narnia book was being prepared for publication in 1952, Tolkien yet remained without a publisher for *The Lord of the Rings*. Jack had almost finished writing the entire Narnia series, seven in all, the biblical number of perfection. Though the books had not been written in chronological order—for instance, the creation of Narnia was told in the sixth book: *The Magician's Nephew*—he had covered Narnia from its creation to the last battle. Jack knew that far from being a hodgepodge of

171

elements, the Narnia series paralleled the truths of Christianity.

"But this won't be evident to grownups for many years to come," he fussed to Warnie. "Of course, the children will know it already."

"Several million, I suspect, from the way the books are selling," predicted Warnie in amazement.

Jack, however, did not gloat over his success or Tolkien's problems. He wasn't that kind of a friend. Besides, he was convinced that *The Lord of the Rings* was a yet unrecognized masterpiece. Instead, Tolkien was the one who had trouble dealing with the situation. He had never seemed more petulant. "I'm sad I can have no sympathy for your Narnia stories," he fretted to Jack.

One morning in September Jack informed Warnie, "Joy Gresham is visiting here in Oxford today."

"Your pen-friend from America!" exclaimed Warnie.

"Come and meet her," Jack urged. "She has invited us both to lunch at the Eastgate Hotel."

In the company of Warnie, Jack felt safe enough. If she was a nuisance, like one woman who had claimed to be his wife, he would make it a short lunch indeed. He felt a very haggard fifty-four. Joy Gresham, a bubbly, witty thirty-seven, made him feel like Methuselah. She was springtime, with large Bette Davis eyes behind horn-rimmed glasses, and full-figured. In some ways she reminded him of Charles Williams, homely until she began talking. Then, to Jack, she transcended her plain features and became angelic.

Her conversation was lively and as irreverent as Hugo Dyson's, and though she flattered Jack in an obvious way, he liked it. Jack admired her for having risen so far above her terrible personal problems. She was spunky, rebellious, full of good-natured exchanges. Jack had never met a woman so like his best friends. She was nearly a perfect companion. Of course he did not mean romantically; he simply meant that her wit and vivacity and shocking frankness made her enjoyable. Even Warnie liked her.

At her first lunch at Magdalen College Jack heard her ask Warnie, "Is there anywhere in this monastic establishment where a lady can relieve herself?"

Because Jack and Warnie liked her bubbly company so much, Jack invited Joy to stay with them at the Kilns during the holidays. After some deliberation, he and Warnie decided they should behave just as they always did: walking, reading, and visiting pubs. A serious writer with several books already published, Joy fit right in, no more disruptive than the irreverent Hugo Dyson, and Jack critiqued the manuscript of her book, *Smoke on the Mountain*, her interpretation of the ten commandments.

Mischievously, Warnie teased Jack in private, "I say, you look rosier-cheeked than you have for years, Small-Piggy-Bottom."

During Joy's visit at the Kilns, she received a letter from her husband, William Gresham, asking for a divorce. Gresham often drank and had a violent temper. By now, Jack knew that he was a writer too, with one very successful book, *Nightmare Alley*. His letter shocked even Joy. He planned to marry her cousin Renee, who would soon get her own divorce, and take in Renee's two children. Gresham informed Joy she was to live nearby with their two boys so he would be able to share raising them.

After she left, Jack stormed, "Joy is going back to face the most selfish man in America. I wonder if we'll ever see her again."

"Does seem rather dreary around here now," commented Warnie.

fourteen

"Letter from Joy," announced Warnie one morning several days later, his anticipation obvious.

Jack read it and sighed. "Her husband is not only living with her cousin Renee, but also is now drunk most of the time."

Both brothers were very relieved when Joy returned to England in February of 1953. Any suggestion that Jack had anything to do with her divorce was squelched when she took up residence in London. She enrolled her boys in a prep school there and lived off royalty from her books and alimony. Jack didn't see her again until Christmas of 1953.

"So these are the boys," he greeted, looking at David, nine, and Douglas, eight.

They were thin, large-eyed boys with furry hair and animal energy. At first they were quiet, but they soon grew restless. Well, Jack decided, since he was quite the walker, he would see that they were kept busy. Almost immediately he took off for Shotover Hill. Warnie and Joy strolled far behind.

"This way, boys, this way," he gestured to them as he left the trail to thrash into bushes. Soon they were marching beside him. When they had exhausted Shotover Hill, they drove into Oxford. Jack showed them the deer behind Magdalen, then took them on Addison's Walk. Finally he let them climb the stairs of Magdalen Tower.

On ground level again, Jack asked, "Well, boys, what did you think of the view?"

"Wonderful," they chirped delightedly. "Let's go up again."

For four days Jack met the challenge, only allowing himself to collapse after Joy and the boys left for London. He had given them a manuscript of *The Horse and His Boy*, his fifth Narnia story, and promised them he would dedicate it to them. He always claimed to be uncomfortable around children, but his only fault was trying too hard to entertain them. He was a child himself in many ways.

After that introduction to the boys, Jack and Joy began seeing each other both in London and Oxford. Many of Jack's colleagues in Oxford were very cool to her, apparently resenting her brashness. Even Tolkien was cool. Since that was his way most of the time, Jack did not hold it against him any more than he did his ruthless honesty, but it stung nonetheless. When Tolkien's first volume of, *The Lord of the Rings—The Fellowship of the Rings* was finally published in 1954, Jack wrote a review and a dust-jacket blurb of highest praise.

"But," he warned Tolkien, "I am much hated now in Oxford and some academic circles. I might do you more harm than good."

Jack may have been right. Reviews of *The Fellowship of the Rings* were universally good. The only negative parts of the reviews were vicious attacks on Jack's comments! Sales were strong, and almost immediately it was obvious that Tolkien had accomplished a major commercial success too. Although he had lived in Jack's shadow as a published writer for years, now Tolkien was on the rise.

That same year Jack's "Oh Hell!" was finally published. It was the third volume of *Oxford History of English Literature*, titled *English Literature in the Sixteenth Century excluding drama*. The very first chapter of the 696-page opus was a shocker. In it, he asserted no less than that the Renaissance as understood never existed in England; that the great flowering of literature in England that had reached its apex in Shakespeare was a separate phenomenon! From there, Jack proceeded to defend the Puritans and damn the humanists. Next he surveyed all the writers of the 16th Century, good and bad. This first chapter alone was bound to make Jack a lightning rod among scholars.

Reviews praised it as they had *The Allegory of Love*. The LTS said:

> *Learned, vivacious. . .a notable perfor-*
> *mance. Few critics of recent years have*
> *brought to the study of English literature so*
> *wide a knowledge both of the classical lit-*
> *eratures and of French and Italian litera-*
> *ture. . .And Mr. Lewis, be it said, knows*
> *how to make his learning felt—you feel,*
> *reading him, that he has read what he is*
> *talking about. Even so, what is best in his*
> *book, perhaps, is the lively, individual*
> *quality of it.*

Academic circles, however, were not as pleased with the book. They attacked it. How dare he promote Christianity and damn humanism in what was supposed to be a scholarly work?

"Wonder of wonders," a very pleased Jack chortled to Warnie, "Tolkien likes it!"

Meanwhile Jack was writing *Surprised by Joy*, the account

176

of his conversion. He related it from his earliest memories of childhood, especially his glimpses of joy, to his final conversion to Christianity on the road to Whipsnade Zoo in 1931. He portrayed Warnie, Mother, Poodaytabird, the public schools, Smewgy, Arthur, Kirk, Sergeant Ayers, Laurence Johnson, Barfield, Coghill, Benecke, and many others. Sometimes the very individuals who moved the plot remained unnamed. He excepted no one but Mrs. Moore, knowing already that to include her would only detract from his story because many refused to believe the mother-son relationship they had shared. He plumbed the depths of Oxford for all his old memories as if purging them because, deep in his heart, he had given up on Oxford.

A movement in the English Department in 1954 to restore Victorian Literature to the curriculum had been the last straw. Years before, Jack had fought alongside Tolkien, at his behest, to successfully remove it. Now to his utter amazement, when Tolkien was in the influential position of full professor, he was waffling. Yes, Tolkien allowed, he might be in favor of restoring Victorian Literature. Jack led a mighty resistance against the restoration and it was defeated, but his disgust with Oxford was complete.

When the English faculty at Cambridge University learned of Jack's unhappiness, they created the chair of Medieval and Renaissance studies specifically for him. Jack had a problem, however. He couldn't afford to purchase another house because the Kilns, which would legally pass on to Maureen, could not be sold. He and Warnie had to keep the Kilns. On the other hand, he couldn't leave Warnie at the Kilns for weeks at a time. Warnie's last binge in August had landed him in a nursing home again. Warnie's book on seventeenth century France, *The Splendid Century*, had been

177

published in 1953 with pleasant reviews, and he was now writing another book. But the binges continued.

Cambridge tactfully bent the rules for Jack. During term Jack would be allowed to return to Oxford for weekends. Though he dreaded the change from Oxford, Jack gave his inaugural lecture at Cambridge November, 1954. The hall was packed. Jack described himself as an Old Western man and expanded on his Medieval Model that reigned to the time of Milton. The audience roared their appreciation. Delighting in the hospitable atmosphere for Christianity, he realized his change had been wise.

"To think," marveled Warnie, "that forty years ago you and Poodaytabird decided Cambridge was the refuge of hard-boiled science."

Almost as if to insult Oxford, Jack had Joy help him move out of his rooms in January of 1955. He used the move to cull his belongings, selling much of his furniture and many of his books. Joy was astounded to discover Jack had already thrown away working manuscripts of his famous books, and even more astounded to find he had no copies of some of the books themselves!

At Cambridge, Jack lived as an ascetic. In each sitting room, he placed only bookcases, a table, and hardback chairs. He refused the loan of sofas and easy chairs to purposely lead an austere life.

He traveled back and forth between Oxford and Cambridge on the slowest train available. The train he dubbed the "crawler" traversed the seventy miles in a very leisurely three hours. Habitually far too early at the station for his departure, he would pace the platform. Then he would select a window seat near the front of the car, alternately gazing at scenery and reading a book.

Occasionally, toting his "pack"—an old khaki rucksack containing rain gear, a lunch of sandwiches, and perhaps cheese—he would ride the train to visit a friend. That the visit would be structured around walks was understood. He and his companion would alternate carrying the pack as they walked. Every half hour or so they would rest. As in the past, arriving at an inn at an appointed hour was very important. A new development, however, rendered some inns most unacceptable. "Just the sight of a jukebox will send me right back out the door," he warned his friends.

Although Jack was much less aggressive in conversations now, one thing had not changed: he still focused conversations entirely outside himself. Topics discussed were literary or ethical conundrums. He thwarted all attempts to pry into his life. When someone became too personal, his face would ice over, his eyes become distant. Nor did he pry himself. Understandably, he repelled gossip immediately, but he also excluded even routine chitchat about his family and friends. The only exceptions were conversations between Jack and Owen Barfield, or Tolkien, or Arthur, or occasionally Warnie.

In 1955, Joy and her sons moved to Headington, only one mile from the Kilns. From that time on, Jack saw her every day that he was back in Oxford. Her younger boy, Doug, remained sunny, but her older boy, David, unable to accept his mother's decision to leave America, had become hostile. To rebel, he insisted on being Jewish although Judaism had never been practiced by either of his parents.

Warnie was still bingeing twice or more a year, ending up in a nursing home each time. Jack wondered how much longer his unhealthy constitution could last.

Then a new problem loomed. Joy learned her work permit

might not be extended. Jack couldn't bear to think of her going back to America and coming under the influence of her violent, immoral ex-husband. There was a solution, a way she could stay in England: he could marry her. Jack agonized over the idea.

One day, with a friend from Oxford, Jack discussed poet Ruth Pitter. Ruth's poetry humbled Jack. After he had read her poetry, which to Jack soared to the heights of Mozart, his own seemed as harsh as a brass band. Then Jack added, "Ruth would be a perfect wife for me."

"It isn't too late," encouraged the friend, stunned by such a personal revelation from Jack.

"Oh, but it is too late." Jack's candor was surprising even himself, but this friend was unfailingly discreet, and he had to have a sounding board. He laid out Joy's whole problem. Then his solution. "We wouldn't live as man and wife," he clarified. "The marriage would just be a formality."

"Not true at all," objected his friend hotly, who seemed to discern that Jack was altogether unsure of the solution. "If anything were to happen to Joy, you would be legally responsible for the two boys."

"Nevertheless, if they refuse to extend her permit, I can't let her go back to America."

In 1955, *Surprised by Joy* was published. Reviews were mixed. Some thought the train of thought unconvincing. Some did not believe reason could lead someone to the gospel. Some thought only a few individuals with Jack's intellect and classical background could follow such an intellectual path.

Some were merely curious. Why was Jack not naming some names? What was he hiding? Where was the dirt? Even friends joked it should instead be titled, *Suppressed by Jack.* Even so, Jack was satisfied that he had explained his conversion precisely the way he remembered it. And the book sold very well.

"You were very harsh on Malvern School," judged Warnie, trying to restrain his anger over an ancient sticking point.

"That's the way I choose to remember Malvern," affirmed Jack of his last public school.

Joy latched on to one of Jack's old ideas and undertook to persuade him to brave a bold direction. Since his under-graduate days, Jack had toyed with and abandoned the myth of Cupid and Psyche. "Why not resurrect it?" she prodded. "Aren't the Narnia stories the perfection of an idea you once abandoned? And look how well they turned out!" As Jack contemplated that the seventh and last of the series would be published in the fall of 1956, he agreed to seriously consider the myth again.

In Roman mythology, the story begins with Venus, god-dess of love, jealous of the mortal princess Psyche's beauty. Venus orders her son, the god Cupid, to make Psyche fall in love with the ugliest man in the world. Instead, Cupid falls in love with Psyche and carries her off to a remote palace where he visits her only by night, unseen and unrecognized by her. He forbids her ever to look at his face, but one night Psyche looks upon him while he sleeps. For disobeying him, Cupid abandons her. Psyche wanders the world in search of him. After many trials, she is reunited with Cupid and is even made immortal by Jupiter, the king of the gods.

With Joy's help, Jack created a new character, Orual, the ugly half-sister of Psyche. The story unravels through her eyes. Orual is the one who persuades Psyche to look at Cupid, thereby causing her to wander the earth. Then using an artifice of the supernatural that Charles Williams used,

Jack has Orual suffer for Psyche. When Psyche and Cupid are reunited, Orual discovers that her sacrifice has redeemed her and that she is now beautiful too. Jack realized worriedly that he had created a plot far more complex than any in the space trilogy. The motives of the ministering angels were formidable to decipher.

"Are you sure it's not too difficult for readers?" Jack pressed Joy.

"You don't always have to write for the lowest common denominator," bantered Joy.

By April 1956, Joy had learned her work permit would not be extended. On April 23, 1956, therefore, Jack and Joy were married in a civil ceremony. Jack insisted it was only a technicality, a necessary requirement so that his good friend could remain safe in England. He told almost no one except Warnie and the discreet friend. Joy remained living in her house in Headington, and they continued the very best of friends. Then Joy, at only forty one, began to suffer aches and pains in her left hip.

"The quacks say it's fibrositis, a weird form of rheumatism," Joy explained to Jack.

Jack's story of Cupid and Psyche, *Till We Have Faces*, came out in the fall of 1956. Critics overwhelmingly admired it. Jack had explored all the meanings of love in a very complex myth. Also, the meaning of the story was not apparent until the very end. Jack's public, on the other hand, was baffled. The story was so difficult to follow, and they had not the patience to pursue it to the end. They did not read "C.S. Lewis" to be mystified. And where was the Christianity? What were they to think? The book sold poorly. In Jack's mind though, *Till We Have Faces* and *Perelandra* were his two best fictions—and who was a better judge of fiction?

"So what if it takes a hundred years or more to discover its merits?" shrugged Jack. "I've never written for money or recognition."

Some of the old Inklings told him in brutal frankness that it was his only truly original work. In all his other works he had imitated a mentor: Bunyan, Chesterton, MacDonald, Williams. *Till We Have Faces* was the true Jack: deeply classical and quite complex, far too complicated for any ordinary reader to comprehend.

To Warnie, Jack expressed disappointment. "I suppressed explicit Christianity, and I didn't mix themes. This should be the one book Tolkien really likes, but I hear nothing from him."

In October Joy fell at her house in Headington and was helpless until found by a neighbor. To Jack's horror, x-rays of Joy revealed the earlier diagnosis of fibrositis was completely wrong. . .

fifteen

Love

Under the cold fluorescent lights of the Wingfield-Morris Hospital, where Joy was now a patient, Jack broke the news to the two boys when they recessed for Christmas vacation. "Your mother's illness is very serious."

"People don't die from a broken leg," snapped David defensively.

"No," murmured Jack. He himself was reeling. His mother, his father, his Aunt Annie. Now Joy. "It's cancer," he told the boys quietly. They looked like he had slapped their faces. Douglas started crying. "Don't give up hope," Jack encouraged. "She has a chance to recover. They're going to operate to remove the cancer."

"Cut out cancer so bad it has eaten though a bone already?" challenged David.

Later, with Warnie, Jack was explicit. "They're transferring her to Churchill Hospital—our local cancer ward. There they'll remove a tumor in her breast as well as the cancerous bone and her ovaries. She has a moderate chance of lingering for a few years, but more likely, she will die in a few months."

"You haven't mentioned her chance for a full recovery. . ." Warnie hoped.

"Less than one percent," Jack unintentionally whispered.

Joy looked it. Her skin was greenish yellow. Dark circles

184

around her large dark eyes made them huge wells of suffering. Yet, who bolstered Jack and the boys? Joy—the dying, owl-eyed victim. Instead of wallowing in self-pity or smoldering in anger at her fate, she attempted to lift the spirits of everyone around her, cracking jokes and pricking every little balloon of pity.

"What pluck," admired Warnie several weeks later. "Surely she is recovering."

"No," negated Jack. "The cancer is only stabilized for a while. Eventually she will have to convalesce at home."

"She can't go back to the house in Headington," insisted Warnie. "We must have her at the Kilns."

"I was hoping to hear you say that. There's another matter to take care of." Jack hesitated.

"We'll care for the boys. . ." Warnie's voice trailed off.

"Yes. I meant something more immediate though. We must publish the marriage in the newspaper so no one will question her right to be at the Kilns."

"Of course," Warnie instantly agreed.

So, the marriage was revealed in the newspaper, but the fact that Jack had kept it secret for several months did nothing to help his relationship with old Oxford friends like Tolkien. Jack, not one to expect others to explain their personal lives, felt no obligation to explain his own. He was interested in issues and morality.

Warnie, thinking to escape trauma by sinking back into the bottle, was soon lost in an alcoholic haze again. Through Christmas of 1956, Jack, with no domestic help, tried to manage the Kilns, Joy's two sons, four geese, ten chickens, a cat and a dog, and a very sick Warnie in bed.

Over the next several months, Jack admitted to himself that he truly loved Joy. Not only was she enduring the severest trial a person can suffer, she was triumphing. Not in physical recovery, but in spirit. He realized God meant her to be his real wife. Yes, she had been married, but that marriage had been profaned by her husband. In the Gospel of Matthew, didn't Jesus Himself say one who divorces because of *adultery* may marry another?

One day in March he confided to Warnie, "The doctors advise me to take her out of the hospital. Nothing is working now, and the expense is crushing."

"It sounds like a death sentence," Warnie sighed.

Jack barely nodded before announcing, "I'm going to marry Joy."

One of Jack's former pupils, the Reverend Peter Bide, married Jack and Joy in her hospital room March 21, 1957. The following week, a full-time nurse was hired, and Joy was installed at the Kilns on the first floor.

In April Jack wrote Arthur that Joy was fading fast. It was only a matter of time. Her mental state was not helped by her ex-husband, who wrote to assert his claim on the boys once she died.

For some time already Jack had been intrigued by a certain phenomenon: a miracle whereby one person actually takes on another's suffering. Charles Williams had insisted it was true. Jack himself had used it in *Till We Have Faces*. Even Tolkien half believed it, once hearing a very convincing story of such substitution from his own dentist. So Jack began to pray for such a thing. One day when Joy's legs ached so intolerably she could no longer hide it and she cried in agony, Jack went off to pray more fervently than ever for God to transfer Joy's pain to him.

"Please God," he begged, "You must let this pain pass to me."

Immediately his legs were seized by discomfort. Then, within only a few short minutes, his legs pulsated with excruciating pain. He kept from screaming only by gritting his teeth. Hours later the pain finally faded. Drained, he hobbled into Joy's room. She smiled. She had not looked so well in a long time.

"Is it my imagination?" he questioned himself. "What if this pain means nothing but sympathy?"

Finding out if Joy actually felt better was hard. She always said she felt better—even as a twitch in her face betrayed a sudden stab of pain. Jack constantly badgered himself wondering if the severe pain he was enduring meant nothing. "Oh, how the devil would enjoy such a trick!" he muttered, exasperated.

Nevertheless, he continued praying, and his prayers seemed answered, because he was becoming very ill. He ached all over all the time as if he had the flu, and occasionally experienced real torment.

One beautiful day Joy's face was clouded in gloom. "You're in pain," he sympathized.

"Not at all," she averred. "I feel no pain at all. You must believe me. But on such a day as this, I want very much to live, and I know it's hopeless."

"A dungeon is never harder to bear than when the door is open and the sunshine and bird song float in," he philosophized. "Nevertheless, Christians always have hope."

Jack continued to suffer mightily himself. "Enough is enough," decreed Jack's old friend and physician, Robert Havard. "Let's get you off to the hospital."

Tests at the hospital revealed Jack was losing calcium. His osteoporosis was remarkable. Baffled, he pondered his condition. *Have I so convinced myself to suffer for Joy that*

C. S. Lewis

I am losing my bones too? For what purpose?

Then the miracle was confirmed. Tests on Joy revealed that her bones were regenerating!

"Praise the Lord," exulted Jack.

By September, Joy, who in April had needed to be lifted onto a bedpan, was walking. Since Jack's osteoporosis was being treated, he was improving too. Incredibly, they seemed to have a future together.

"Well, dearest, now we can have some relaxed days together," promised a cheery Jack.

"Not on your life," Joy contradicted.

Jack's brow furrowed. "Whatever do you mean?"

"I mean the house, dear," Joy lilted.

"I'm not sure we can afford. . ."

"You can't afford not to," she interrupted.

The Kilns had suffered greatly from the war and the rationing after the war. Because coal had been in short supply, the house had never been kept warm enough. The resultant moisture had bubbled and flaked off the wallpaper. Mrs. Moore had been too ill to do anything about it; Jack and Warnie had chosen to ignore it as unimportant. Much more inconvenient was never having a hot bath. And sleeping in a room so cold that the water in the wash basin froze during the night!

Joy made her point in an unusually tactful manner. "The light switches sting my fingers like wasps. The floors are rotting under these thirty-year-old carpets. The roof leaks. We are in danger of plaster falling on our heads."

"That bad?" queried Jack, looking up. "I say, there is rather a bad water spot up there. I never noticed."

"With your permission. . ." Joy tilted her head to one side.

"Certainly, dear, if you're willing to spearhead the thing.

Yes," Jack suddenly was convinced, "it's just the thing!"

For weeks the Kilns swarmed with electricians, plumbers, carpenters, painters, and decorators. A central heating system was installed. The kitchen, no longer archaic, boasted a modern gas stove. The transformation was incredible. Even Jack noticed it. Had the house really been that shabby?

"Next I go outside," planned Joy, now moving around very ably with a cane.

"Outside?" questioned Jack. "Surely you don't think the outside needs renovation?"

Hedges were trimmed, flowers were planted, trellises were repaired for climbing roses, and Joy discovered their worst eyesore. Their pond and woods had become a gathering place for adolescents at night, and the boys and girls were not smelling flowers and reading poetry to each other. They were drinking alcohol, stealing wood, and worse. Was Jack not aware of it?

"We can't keep them out." Jack, gentle old pacifist that he was, shrugged his shoulders. His opinion of Joy's remedy for the situation was, "It seems uncharitable of us."

"It's certainly not Christian charity to provide the site for sin," she argued pointedly. "And what about our two boys?"

"Yes, you're right. We'll go ahead with your plan."

Joy's plan was successful. After many warnings were scorned, a couple of shotgun blasts high over the heads of the trespassers discouraged them from returning. Once again Jack and Warnie possessed all of their acreage. Now David and Douglas could roam the grounds without being threatened or stumbling into sin.

Jack, quickly assured that he need not travel to America, was invited by Christian radio in America to record a series of talks for Americans. Given his choice of topics, he selected the four loves: *eros*, *philia*, *storge*, and, the only virtuous form, *agape*. He immediately began writing his scripts. His relationship with Joy had crystallized his thoughts on love. As he had freely shared in a letter to a friend, his love for Joy had begun with *agape*, or Christian charity. Then it had grown to include *philia*, the undemanding love between friends. Later, *eros*, physical love, had developed. *Agape* seemed to have incarnated for Jack. He was quite struck by that.

"Who would have thought I would possess at nearly sixty, what I was denied at twenty and thirty?" he marveled to Owen Barfield.

He had already finished the manuscript of a work on the Psalms which explained much of the rest of the Old Testament as well. The purpose was to help Christians deal with certain Old Testament attitudes that seemed not only un-Christian but barbaric. How does one justify cursing enemies and delighting in their slaughter? How does one deal with a religion that barely mentions life hereafter? Jack, however, praised the enormous exuberance of the Jews— their love of natural law grounded in their mighty God.

"It's virtually the same theism that I held for two years on my path to Christ," he described to Joy.

Joy's cancer was in complete remission. By July of 1958 both Joy and Jack were so healthy again—even taking one-mile walks—that Jack decided she must see Ireland. Because a sea voyage was too risky—a fall by either one of them would be disastrous, for the first time in his life Jack traveled by plane.

After a terrifying take-off that seemed to him like the launch of a rocket ship, he relaxed. The glorious cloudscape mesmerized him. Once in Ireland, Arthur chauffeured them about in his car. For two weeks Jack delighted in Joy discovering the blue mountains and yellow shores of Ireland.

Warnie still disappeared on binges. More and more he ended up in Ireland because Lourdes Hospital in Drogheda showed inexhaustible patience with his drinking. Around Oxford's convalescent centers, he had become a pariah. Yet his productivity while sober was astonishing. He typed all Jack's correspondence, besides having written three full-fledged and well-reviewed books on French history.

Another reason behind Warnie's Irish destination was Joy's presence at the Kilns. She wielded a very sharp tongue, but, more importantly, Warnie did not like to disappoint her. He knew she had suffered more than enough under one drunk.

That fall of 1958, Jack's book, *Reflections on the Psalms*, was enthusiastically received by the public. A religious book in hard cover selling 11,000 copies before release was remarkable. Although the critics were less enthusiastic than the public, one of the most complimentary reviews came from Jack's favorite, the LTS, which proclaimed:

> *Professor Lewis. . .gives less attention than one might have expected to the literary quality of the Psalms and none at all to the circumstances in which they were composed. But he retains that habit of working out Christian ideas to their logical conclusion which so annoys his opponents, and his comment is enlightening, heartening, and full of penetrating moral insight. This book may not tell the reader all he would like to know about the Psalms, but it will tell him a good deal he will not like to know about himself. . .*

Other critics emphasized its lack of scholarship, apparently oblivious to Jack's explanation in the introduction that it was from a layman's point of view. "As a literary critic myself," he griped to Joy, "it pains me to endure careless reviews."

His radio talks on the "four loves" inspired him to expand on the subject for a book. Everything seemed back to normal, even better than normal. Had he or Joy ever relished life so much as now? They completed a second trip to Ireland in the summer of 1959. Then they planned a trip for 1960 that Joy had always craved: the isles of Greece. Agreeing to this trip was quite a concession by Jack. He loathed foreign travel—even to a favorite place in literature.

"Don't you see," he implored, "the drab reality could destroy the golden image in my imagination!" Nevertheless, he assured Joy he would go to Greece in 1960.

Joy was ebullient when she went for routine x-rays in October of 1959. For the first time she did not dread the results. She was certain that she was well. . .

sixteen

Grief

The cancer was back!

"It was as if Joy and I had escaped the Giant," Jack numbly told Warnie later, "and now we've been recaptured just as the castle is almost out of sight!"

The first escape had been a miracle. Could they escape again? And could Jack's faith remain intact? To sympathetic friends, Jack tried to be as cheerful as Joy. "Yes," Jack assured those who questioned, "no matter what happens, we are indeed grateful to God for the miracle that allowed us two active years together." But deep inside he was fighting his own ugly black cancer: doubt. . .

He spent as much time with Joy as he could and determined that as long as she was alive he would make her happy. Making her happy meant that, sick or not, she wanted to go to Greece. So, there in April of 1960, Joy tried very hard to see the ancient glories. She actually climbed up the Acropolis, strolled with Jack through the streets of the village of Lindos, and reached the Lion Gate at Mycenae.

One particular day, April 6, seemed perfection to Jack- one of the supreme days of his life. They left Athens in a car with a guide to cross Mount Cithaeron and descend through pine woods and olive groves to the Bay of Corinth. At Aegosthena, with the azure bay of Homer and Plato glistening in front of them, they whiled away the hours sipping "retsina" and eating Mediterranean delicacies.

Jack acknowledged to Joy, "Never in my life have I experienced absolute contentment—until this moment."

By the end of the trip, however, Joy was drinking heavily to smother her pain. Within days of their return to Oxford, she underwent surgery to remove cancer from her breast. She seemed to rebound, once again returning to the Kilns, but recovery was only temporary. By the middle of June, she began failing very rapidly and returned to the hospital. By sheer will power, she seemed to recover again, returning to the Kilns with enough pluck to play "Scrabble." On the morning of July 13, however, she screamed in agony.

Back in the hospital that afternoon, heavily drugged yet lucid, Joy advised Jack, "Don't buy me a fancy coffin. Fancy coffins are all rot." During the late evening, she assured Jack that he had made her very happy. Then she told a chaplain she was at peace with God. Minutes later, she died. To Jack, who had seen so many violent deaths, her dying seemed very natural.

Joy wished to be cremated, her dust scattered. There would be no memorial other than a plaque at the Oxford Crematorium. The day of her funeral was bright and sunny. The complete absence of Jack's friends was chilling. Later he wrote his friends brave letters that said, "We enjoyed the fruits of a miracle. I'm not sure it would. . .[be] right to ask for another." Regardless, the reality of his dismal, confused circumstances grew.

Jack started a journal to record his turmoil. At first he praised his beloved:

> *Her mind was lithe and quick and muscular*
> *as a leopard. Passion, tenderness, and pain*
> *were equally unable to disarm it. It scented*

its first whiff of cant or slush; then sprang,
and knocked you over before you knew what
was happening. . .I soon learned not to talk
rot to her. . .[1]

Thoughts turned to his own lack of drive:

Except at my job-where the machine seems
to run on much as usual-I loathe the slight-
est effort. . .Even shaving. . .It's easy to see
why the lonely become untidy. . .[2]

The self-confident apologist became acutely self-conscious:

I cannot talk to the children about her. The
moment I try, there appears on their faces
. . .the most fatal of all non-conductors,
embarrassment. . .I felt just the same after
my own mother's death when my father
mentioned her. . .It's the way boys are. . .It
isn't only the boys either. An odd by-prod-
uct of my loss is that I'm aware of embar-
rassment to everyone I meet. I see people,
as they approach me, trying to make up
their minds whether they'll "say something
about it" or not. I hate it if they do, and if
they don't. . .Perhaps the bereaved ought
to be isolated in special settlements like
lepers. . .[3]

And finally the confusion and embarrassment sought the
ultimate cause:

> *Oh God, God, why did you take such trouble*
> *to force this creature out of its shell if it is*
> *now doomed to crawl back—to be sucked*
> *back—into it?. . .*[4]

His torment changed to anger:

> *Meanwhile where is God?. . .When you are*
> *happy, so happy that you have no sense*
> *of needing Him. . .you will be—or so it*
> *feels—welcomed with open arms. But go to*
> *Him when your need is desperate, when all*
> *other help is in vain, and what do you*
> *find? A door slammed in your face, and a*
> *sound of bolting and double bolting on the*
> *inside. After that, silence. . .*[5]

He argued with himself, the apologist of old:

> *Not that I am (I think) in much danger of*
> *ceasing to believe in God. The real danger*
> *is of coming to believe such dreadful*
> *things about Him. . ."So this is what God's*
> *really like. Deceive yourself no longer."*[6]

His thoughts became uglier:

> *Sooner or later I must face the question in*
> *plain language. What reason have we,*
> *except our own desperate wishes, to believe*
> *that God is. . . "good"? Doesn't all* prima
> facie *evidence suggest exactly the oppo-*
> *site?. . .(What if Christ) were mistaken?. . .*

("Why hast Thou forsaken me?")...may
have a perfectly clear meaning...[7]

He wallowed in introspection—the one thing he had
avoided for years:

It's not true that I'm always thinking of
(Joy). Work and conversation make that
impossible. But...there is spread over
everything a vague sense...of wrongness
...What's...wrong? Then I remember...
We were even told, "Blessed are they that
mourn," and I accepted it...Of course, it
is different when the thing happens to one-
self, not to others...If I had really cared,
as I thought I did, about the sorrows of the
world, I should not have been so over-
whelmed when my own sorrow came...if
my house was a house of cards, the sooner
it was knocked down the better...(if a
"restoration of faith")...happens I shan't
know if it is (another house of cards)...
until the next blow comes...[8]

Then he would scold himself for being so self-absorbed.
What was his suffering compared to Joy's?

What is grief compared to physical pain?...
physical pain can be absolutely continuous
...like the steady barrage on a trench in
World War I, hours of it with no let-up for a
moment...[9]

Slowly he justified suffering, even if one cannot understand it at the time:

> . . .suppose. . .(God is like a). . .surgeon
> whose intentions are wholly good. . .The
> kinder he is. . .the more inexorably he will
> go on cutting. . .If he yields to (our cries to
> stop). . .all the pain up to that point would
> have been useless. But is it credible that
> such extremities of torture should be nec-
> essary for us? Well, take your choice. . .If
> they are unnecessary, then there is no God
> or a bad one. . .[10]

Finally Jack saw a ray of sunlight:

> Something quite unexpected happened. . .
> this morning. . .my heart was lighter than
> it had been for many weeks. . .and when,
> so far, I mourned (Joy) the least, I remem-
> bered her the best. . .It was as if the lifting
> of the sorrow removed a barrier. . .[11]

And Jack began to see his intense mourning denied the love he should be giving God:

> (Joy). . .and all the dead are. . .(remote)
> . . .like God. In that respect loving her has
> become, in its measure, like loving Him. . .
> there's no practical problem before me at all.
> I know the two great commandments, and I'd
> better get on with them. . .While she was alive
> I could, in practice, put her before God. . .[12]

And, regaining his first priority, God, after many weeks, he felt the presence of his wife for the first time:

> *. . .last night's experience. . .was quite incredibly unemotional. Just the impression of her mind momentarily facing my own. . .*
> *Not at all like a rapturous reunion of lovers. . .*
> *(but). . .intimacy that had not passed though the senses or the emotions. . .(yet). . .complete-sharply bracing. . .(If that is the love of the world beyond) how many preconceptions I must scrap! (The world beyond is not emotional but). . .solid. Utterly reliable. Firm. There is no nonsense. . .*[13]

At last Jack could now think what had been unthinkable. He would not call Joy back even if he had the power to do so:

> *How wicked it would be, if we could, to call the dead back! She said. . ."I am at peace with God."* [14]

Eventually he sent his journal to the publisher Faber and Faber. How could he deny others who might be grieving a history of his own grief and recovery? It could help them cope. All the same, he decided to use a pen-name: N.W. Clerk. He had good reasons. First of all, he did not want to undermine the air of certainty in his other books about God. Secondly, he felt obligated to answer all serious letters. And thirdly, he could not bear the thought of answering the hundreds of letters that would pour in.

He had to get on with his life. His weight had dropped from 200 pounds to 170 pounds. He was responsible for the two boys. William Gresham had come to England shortly after Joy had died, but surprisingly he had made no demands. He had wanted only to console the boys. They had seemed just as embarrassed by his consoling as Jack's.

Meanwhile, in intervals of escape from his grief, Jack had finished two books for 1961: *An Experiment in Criticism* and *Studies in Words*. *An Experiment in Criticism* attacked the growing tendency among even serious scholars to form opinions not after having read the original works but after consulting mere critiques of original works. He had to defend good reading itself:

> *We realize it best when we talk with an unliterary friend. He may be full of goodness and good sense, but he inhabits a tiny world. . .In reading great literature, I become a thousand men. . .*[15]

For obvious reasons, the book was coolly received by critics. On the other hand, critics liked *Studies in Words*. The LTS called it "weighty." The *New York Times* agreed:

> *Rarely is so much learning displayed with so much grace and charm. My only regret is that the book is not twice as long. . .*

The general public had adored *Four Loves*. Too anti-Freudian for intellectuals, it had received a very mixed reception in late 1960 by critics who seemed to think Jack had just pulled his four loves out of the air. How could one understand love without modern psychoanalysis, they wondered. Now, though, the public showed no interest whatsoever in either of his latest books.

Jack faced a more immediate problem, however. His own health was failing.

seventeen

Homecoming

"Your prostate is enlarged, Jack," reported his physician, Robert Havard. "You need surgery."

The surgeon had other ideas though, because Jack was not strong enough to risk surgery. Toxemia from infected kidneys instigated an irregular heart beat. The cure was antibiotics and a special low-protein diet. He was advised to sleep upright in a chair. Worst of all, he was told not to return to Cambridge for the fall term.

"Or perhaps for any term?" he grumbled. He felt very sick and tired.

Nevertheless he attacked his writing. Would he ever be so sick he could not write? He wanted to unite all his lectures on Medieval and Renaissance literature between two covers and title it *The Discarded Image*. He also wanted to write a book on prayer. Thus, late in 1962, he began writing *Letters to Malcolm*. His health began to improve. By the spring of 1962, he resumed his trips to Cambridge on the "crawler." He still felt sick, but activity lifted his spirits.

"God willing, I might even have the prostate operation and completely recover."

That fall he had to tell the two boys very disturbing news from America. Their father had developed cancer of the tongue. Rather than endure what would be a horribly prolonged and painful death, he had committed suicide. So Jack was the boys' last hope. Thank God, he could provide for their education. He already had it all set up with Owen Barfield.

By the spring of 1963, friends commented that Jack looked his old self. His health was so improved that Warnie left for Ireland. Jack planned a trip there himself in July with seventeen-year-old Douglas helping him out.

One day in June, however, he told Douglas, "You had better call Doctor Havard. I feel very ill."

His kidneys were the cause. He was rushed to the hospital for dialysis. The next thing he knew he was talking to friends sometime later. The gist of their conversation was that he had been in a coma. But hadn't he been talking to Charles Williams' wife? Why was she hiding an important unpublished manuscript under her mattress? Hadn't he just talked to Mrs. Moore? Finally it dawned on him that he had been hallucinating. From the drugs? Or perhaps he was only partially out of his coma?

"Where is Warnie?" he asked.

Then he remembered Warnie was in Ireland, drying out at Lourdes from his latest binge. Letters to Warnie informing him Jack was ill went unanswered. Jack was angry thinking how Warnie collapsed in every crisis. A young American, Walter Hooper, was eager to help Jack. Because Jack was mainly concerned about the Kilns, he asked Hooper to move in. Then Jack took a giant step—backward. He resigned his position at Cambridge. Why deny opportunity to someone else? He could remember well enough waiting desperately for a position to open up. He was no hypocrite. Hooper and Douglas retrieved Jack's belongings from Cambridge.

"God, why did I recover from the coma? What is left to do?" Jack wondered day by day. Not for the first time he admired the unsung heroics of Lazarus, who Christ raised

203

from the dead. Before, he had written:

> *But was [Stephen] the first martyr, who*
> *Gave up no more than life, while you,*
> *Already free among the dead,*
> *Your rags stripped off, your fetters shed,*
> *Surrendered what all other men*
> *Irrevocably keep, and when*
> *Your battered ship at anchor lay*
> *Seemingly safe in the dark bay*
> *No ripple stirs, obediently*
> *Put out a second time to sea*
> *Well knowing that your death (in vain*
> *Died once) must be all died again?*[1]

By September Jack was back in the Kilns, reading all his favorites: Homer, Plato, Virgil, Dante, George Herbert, and more. He was feeling better. When Hooper had to return to America, Jack especially wished Warnie would come home from Ireland. "If it weren't for all the letters I have to answer, I could do very well without Warnie!" he complained, exasperated.

Finally Warnie returned. Never had Jack been so glad to see his pear-shaped, apple-cheeked brother, face dark and shiny with a barroom tan. Perhaps this delay by Warnie was best after all. Perhaps Warnie would now be able to resist drinking for a good long time while Jack really needed him.

The two brothers became close again, and talk turned to Boxen and Wynyard and Malvern—the good and bad, the beautiful and ugly. With Warnie there, Jack's old bogies didn't matter.

"Life is pleasant enough now, winding down," he consoled himself. To Warnie he urged, "See that the boys are all right, won't you?" Then he added nonchalantly, "As for me, I want to rest at the Holy Trinity Church."

Jack chuckled, seeing Warnie so gloomy. "Do you remember something you told me years ago about biographies?"

"No," Warnie shook his head.

"You're being polite now, I suspect. But you said biographies make miserable reading toward the end—money problems, deaths of old friends and family, failing health. . ."

"Men must endure their going hence," muttered Warnie.

"Exactly," Jack agreed.

Tolkien visited. "We're like old trees losing our leaves one by one, Jack," he illustrated. Then he became the old Tolkien— brutally honest. "Seeing you like this, Jack, is an ax blow near my roots."

Jack was very sleepy now, almost all the time. Only on rare occasions, like talking with old friends like Tolkien, could he stay awake for quite a long time. Usually he read his glorious books at the Kilns and drowsed. Was there anything more delicious this side of heaven? Perhaps facing a blank sheet of paper, pen in hand, was just as delicious, but he no longer burned with the fire to write. His Christian duty was done. It was time to be judged.

He allowed himself a very rare retrospective: fourteen novel-sized pieces of prose fiction, wasn't it? A number of short stories, and how many lyrical to long narrative poems? His works of imagination totaled a million words probably. His apologetics ran toward a million words too, he supposed. Then there was his academic work, another million words more or less. Including how many essays? More than a hundred? And introductions to other works? Hard to remember. And who was to say the 10,000 or

20,000 letters he had written with a clear head and a mission were not a legacy?

"Why, I have nothing else to say, to be sure!" he persuaded himself.

On November 22, 1963, he was just one week short of his sixty-fifth birthday. Not that it mattered much to him. Not where he was going. Time was a thing peculiar to the material world. Jack was now more tired than ever. It seemed he had been sleeping all day. Warnie woke him up in his easy chair after lunch and advised him politely to go lie on his bed for a nap. At four o'clock, Warnie brought him tea. Fair enough. How often had he brought Warnie tea? Or picked him off the floor? Warnie talked cheerily about his latest book on French history. Jack felt proud of Warnie. Yes, he was flawed, the poor wretch—like all of us—but he did grand things in his sober moments. He had helped Jack enormously, never complaining overmuch—for a brother. Jack thought of all those years with Mrs. Moore's haranguing, remembering that Warnie scarcely complained although Jack knew he had been fuming inside. Having a brother like that was nice. Jack had heard that the sisters in Droghela surmised that Warnie was much more devout than he let on. That was important. Warnie was saved. So was Jack. There just wasn't much left for Jack to do. . .

"Rest up, Small-Piggy-Bottom," teased Warnie as he left the room.

Golden light flooded the room. It was five-thirty, time for Jack to enter that precious otherness for which he had always longed.

ACKNOWLEDGMENTS

Barbour & Company, Inc. expresses their appreciation to all those who generously gave permission to reprint copyrighted material. Diligent effort has been made to identify, locate, contact, and secure permission to use copyrighted material. If any permissions or acknowledgments have been inadvertently omitted or if such permissions were not received by the time of publication, the publisher would sincerely appreciate receiving complete information so that correct credit can be given in future editions.

Chapter 2
[1]Excerpts from "Tegner's Drapa", taken from *The Poetical Works of Longfellow* by Henry Longfellow. Houghton Mifflin, 1975.

Chapter 3
[1]Excerpts from *Boxen: the Imaginary World of the Young C.S. Lewis* by C.S. Lewis and C.S. Lewis's letter to Owen Barfied of 27th May 1928. Reproduced by permission of Curtis Brown Limited, London.
[2]Excerpts from *C.S. Lewis: A Biography* by Roger L. Green and Walter Hooper. Reprinted by permission of Harcourt Brace & Company.

Chapter 4
[1]Excerpts from *Spirits in Bondage* by William Heinemann. Reprinted by permission of Harcourt Brace & Company.
[2]Excerpts from *Letters of C.S. Lewis* by C.S. Lewis, copyright 1966 by W.H. Lewis and the Executors of C.S. Lewis and renewed 1994 by C.S. Lewis Pte Ltd. Reprinted by permission of Harcourt Brace & Company.

Chapter 5
[1]Excerpts from *Spirits in Bondage* by William Heinemann. Reprinted by permission of Harcourt Brace & Company.

Chapter 6
[1]Excerpts from *Letters of C.S. Lewis* by C.S. Lewis, copyright 1966 by W.H. Lewis and the Executors of C.S. Lewis and renewed 1994 by C.S. Lewis Pte Ltd. Reprinted by permission of Harcourt Brace & Company.
[2]Ibid
[3]Ibid

Chapter 7
[1]Excerpts from *Letters of C.S. Lewis* by C.S. Lewis, copyright 1966 by W.H. Lewis and the Executors of C.S. Lewis and renewed 1994 by C.S. Lewis Pte Ltd. Reprinted by permission of Harcourt Brace & Company.
[2]Ibid

Chapter 8
[1]Excerpts from *All My Road Before Me: the diary of C.S. Lewis from 1922-1927* edited by Walter Hooper. Reprinted by permission of Harcourt Brace & Company.
[2]Excerpts from *Clive Staples Lewis: A Dramatic Life* by William Griffin. Harper & Row, 1986.
[3]Excerpts from *Letters of C.S. Lewis* by C.S. Lewis, copyright 1966 by W.H. Lewis and the Executors of C.S. Lewis and renewed 1994 by C.S. Lewis Pte Ltd. Reprinted by permission of Harcourt Brace & Company.
[4]Ibid

Chapter 9
[1]Excerpts from *Letters of C.S. Lewis* by C.S. Lewis, copyright 1966 by W.H. Lewis and the Executors of C.S. Lewis and renewed 1994 by C.S. Lewis Pte Ltd. Reprinted by permission of Harcourt Brace & Company.

[2]Ibid

[3]Excerpts from "Poema Historiale" by Humphrey Carpenter. Taken from *The Inklings*. Houghton Mifflin Company, 1979. Reprinted by permission of Houghton Mifflin Company. Canadian permission to reprint granted by HarperCollins Ltd.

Chapter 10

[1]Excerpt from "Queen of Drum" in *Narrative Poems* by C.S. Lewis, copyright 1969 by C.S. Lewis Pte Ltd, Preface copyright 1969 by Walter Hooper. Reprinted by permission of Harcourt Brace & Company.

[2]Excerpts from "Planets", taken from *C.S. Lewis: Poems* by C.S. Lewis, copyright 1964 by the Executors of the Estate of C.S. Lewis Pte Ltd. And Walter Hooper. Reprinted by permission of Harcourt Brace & Company.

[3]Excerpts from *Letters of C.S. Lewis* by C.S. Lewis, copyright 1966 by W.H. Lewis and the Executors of C.S. Lewis and renewed 1994 by C.S. Lewis Pte Ltd. Reprinted by permission of Harcourt Brace & Company.

[4]Ibid

Chapter 11

[1]Excerpts from *The Price of Success* by J. B. Phillips. Harold Shaw Publishers, 1984. Reprinted by permission of Harold Shaw Publishers. (ch. 11)

Chapter 12

[1]Excerpts from "To Charles Williams", taken from *C.S. Lewis: Poems* by C.S. Lewis, copyright 1964 by the Executors of the Estate of C.S. Lewis Pte Ltd. And Walter Hooper. Reprinted by permission of Harcourt Brace & Company.

[2]Excerpts from *Essays Presented to Charles Williams*. Oxford University Press, 1947. Reprinted by permission of Oxford University Press.

[3]Ibid

Chapter 16

[1]Excerpts from *A Grief Observed* by C.S. Lewis. Copyright 1961 by N.W. Clerk. Reprinted by permission of HarperCollins Publishers Inc. Canadian permission to reprint granted by Faber and Faber Ltd.

[2]Ibid
[3]Ibid
[4]Ibid
[5]Ibid
[6]Ibid
[7]Ibid
[8]Ibid
[9]Ibid
[10]Ibid
[11]Ibid
[12]Ibid
[13]Ibid
[14]Ibid

[15]Excerpts from *An Experiment in Criticism* by C. S. Lewis. Cambridge University Press, 1961. Reprinted by permission of Cambridge University Press.

Chapter 17

[1]Excerpts from "Stephen to Lazarus", taken from *C.S. Lewis: Poems* by C.S. Lewis, copyright 1964 by the Executors of the Estate of C.S. Lewis Pte Ltd. And Walter Hooper. Reprinted by permission of Harcourt Brace & Company.